Beyond Brochures

A Guide for Travellers, their Advisors and Tales from the Road.

by John Picken

 FriesenPress

Suite 300 - 990 Fort St
Victoria, BC, V8V 3K2
Canada

www.friesenpress.com

ISBN
978-1-5255-8878-5 (Hardcover)
978-1-5255-8877-8 (Paperback)
978-1-5255-8879-2 (eBook)

1. TRAVEL, ESSAYS & TRAVELOGUES

Distributed to the trade by The Ingram Book Company

TABLE OF CONTENTS

INTRODUCTION

A FEW winters ago, I had a smart-looking and intelligent young fellow drop by my office. He was heading to Europe in the spring and wanted to talk to someone about the trip. It was to be his honeymoon. He had two weeks and he and his new wife wanted to see Amsterdam, visit family in Slovenia, do a day trip to Venice, and head to Greece for some sun and fun. He had already booked his flight using Aeroplan, flying into and out of Amsterdam. We talked for a few moments before his bride-to-be came in and hurried him on to her next destination. I told him to call if he got a chance. I had a few ideas and I'd like to help. I'm afraid I never saw or heard from him again.

I told a few people about this encounter and how frustrated I was that the fellow hadn't come to a Travel Advisor before he booked his flight. There were a number of things we could have done to save him a lot of time and maybe even some cash. One of my friends in the industry said she could write a whole book about this type of frustrating thing. She didn't, so I decided to do it myself, and now that I'm retired, I've found the time to do it!

Travellers and Travel Advisors are on either side of the same transaction and both need to know how to prepare for and enjoy travel. Since mutual understanding is a good thing, I've put both views into this one book.

As a traveller, you can walk into any travel store and see racks of brochures about travel services available to all travellers. Yet, the best source of great information and real help in arranging a trip of a lifetime is sitting right in front of you, just waiting to be asked for help. Yes, we're in an era of the internet and do-it-yourself travel planning. That's not necessarily a bad thing, but to quote that old, cold warrior Don Rumsfeld, "…there are things we don't know we don't know."

For Travel Advisors, things are changing. The job is no longer a simple clerical function as it might have been in the good old days. Today, a true travel professional uses a well-developed set of skills, knowledge, and practices to create different or unique travel experiences that can never be found on a shelf. As an ex-practitioner and still keen observer of the industry, I wrote this book in an attempt to help both sides of the equation adapt. The more people travel intelligently the better the world should be.

The third and final section is a series of personal observations and ruminations from my own travel experiences for your enjoyment.

A few quick notes before we begin:

This was written for Advisors and clients of leisure-oriented travel agencies. Corporate travel is a whole different business.

It is written for the Canadian market. There are some significant differences between the Canadian and the US travel market.

This was written during the time of the Corona virus. Much may change over the short term but most of what's included should survive over the longer term.

Regardless of whether you're a traveller or an Advisor, feel free to read the whole book. There are no secrets.

Please enjoy.

SECTION A
TRAVELLERS

1.
WHY WE TRAVEL

SHOULD WE travel? Do we really need a reason to travel? What good comes from travel? Some people never travel and never feel the need. Many people can't afford to travel so stay close to home. Yet, much of the world moves around and explores our planet to enjoy themselves and life around them. Generally, people travel for their own reasons. They are motivated to try something new or to explore old haunts in ways that enrich their lives and give it meaning. We can read and watch videos about our world but that will never be as powerful as being there ourselves.

What people do when they travel may give us a hint as to why they do it:

- We want to see where we come from and understand the history and experience the culture that helped make us who we are.

- The beauty of nature attracts a lot of us. We all like to share that view and see the wonders that surround us.

- We like to be entertained or to entertain others.

- We want to meet people who have lives that are different than ours, as it opens our minds to options and opportunities.

- We like to eat different foods and sample different drinks and spend time with those who make them.

- We like to participate in competition, sports, and outdoor activites.

- We travel to foster and celebrate a romance or relationship or family.

- We travel for the sake of our health.

- Travel makes our thinking more sophisticated as we see other ways of behaving and thinking.

- Travel brings different people and different approaches to thinking about our lives and thus sparks creativity.

I think the answer comes when people freely see, understand, mix with, talk to, and watch how others really are. It makes it much more difficult to hate them. We all want to live our lives peacefully. If we let it work on us, travel helps make a peaceful world.

2.
ANTICIPATION, EXPERIENCE, AND MEMORIES

WHAT WAS the best vacation or travel experience you ever had?

When you returned home, could you remember what you were thinking before you left on a trip? Maybe not, but you will remember the pleasure and excitement you felt about the upcoming trip.

However, I bet you can recall many of the details of the trip itself. You can remember the things you did, the things you saw, heard, tasted or tickled your other senses, and the things you felt about the trip.

The *anticipation*, the *experience* and the *memories* are the key stages of any real personal travel. If the memories are to stay with you for a lifetime, the experience needs to go beyond your anticipations. It's the job of your personal Travel Advisor to help make that happen.

A truly professional Travel Advisor concentrates on designing an experience that is everything that you anticipated and then some. Your experience should be more than just the logistics of flights, hotels and other reservations. Your Advisor should help you design the experiences you want and those things that excite your senses, then build the trip around those requirements.

Most experienced Travel Advisors know a lot about travel and are experts in specific destinations and travel specialties. Don't expect them to know everything about everywhere. They know specific regions and destinations and specialties. They travel to their specialty destinations and stay current on their expertise. If they don't know something they know where to go to get the information. Does this mean you may want to have the contacts for a few different Advisors for specific specialties or destinations you want to visit? Maybe, but ask your chosen Advisor for help first!

Is this something that only luxury style travellers can afford? The short answer is no. In fact, a good Advisor is totally concerned that you get value for your travel dollar, regardless of how many of them you have to spend. Like many equations, there are two sides, what you get and what you spend. A top-notch Advisor doesn't focus on one side only; they make sure that they are in sync, plus a little bit more for you! One star or five stars; they want you to enjoy your vacation.

Will this service cost you more? No. They may charge a service fee but it is more than covered by the additional value they add to your travels. They may in fact save you some money. Find a good one, and you'll know the difference between a valued Travel Advisor and a travel booking engine.

3.
IN THE AGE OF THE INTERNET, WHY WOULD ANYONE USE A TRAVEL ADVISOR?

CONSIDER!

The internet offers lots of information and opinions. A Travel Advisor can give you cogent information, time-tested advice, access to supplier assistance, and judgment and wisdom based on years of experience. They've been there, done that; over and over again.

The internet allows you to spend as much time as you want researching a trip. Since you already have a full life, with things like jobs, household chores and family responsibilities, you may find it a little too much. A true travel professional saves you enormous amounts of time. After only a few minutes with you, they can plan and book the entire trip for you, leaving you with nothing to do but to live your life to the full.

The travel industry is constantly changing. Do you have the time to keep up or the background to understand the implications of what's recently happened?

The internet is great at finding a low price. A travel professional can find you great value. You know the difference. Good value is a positive measure of what you get for the price you pay. After all, discounted garbage is still garbage.

Stress is the result of dealing with a new problem, where you're unsure of the outcome. Letting a true expert handle your travel needs eliminates the uncertainty and the problem of not knowing what you don't know. After all, answering specific questions is a whole lot better than providing FAQs!

Doing it yourself means that if unforeseen problems occur, you're pretty much on your own. If you use the services of a competent travel professional you have a friend, someone who can help you out when the world stops working properly. It also means you have the backstop of a provincial regulatory agency (if your province is one of the three that has one: Ontario, BC and Quebec). They are there to protect your travel investment.

4.
LET'S TALK TRAVEL VALUE

'**VALUE, LIKE** beauty, is in the eye of the beholder'. Determining what travel components are valuable is up to the traveller. We all look for things that are interesting and enjoyable for us when we travel. However, for most of us, there's a limit on how much value we can afford, in resources or time.

Normally, we each must decide what we'll spend on this or not spend on that. A Travel Adviser needs to know what is valuable to you and what isn't. Do you want to spend all your time here or over there? Do you want luxury or just comfort or are you willing to rough it?

Best value is not the lowest price or the highest price. It's where and what you want to spend for the time and money you have to spend. As a traveller it's your judgment to make. Some travellers are quite happy to take an off-the-shelf package tour right out of the brochure. It works for them and they feel it's exactly what they want. Others want to visit a remote and exotic location that takes time, specialists, money and effort to visit. Most people understand the value of a hotel on Italy's Amalfi Coast in July is a different proposition than the same place in February!

A Travel Advisor takes this information and converts it into specific decisions you'll need to make.

- How much time do you have for your travel?
- Are you a Four Seasons person or are you happy to use Motel 6?
- Do you always go business class for your flights or are you happy to be at the back of the Airbus?
- Do you want to travel in a group or as a single?

- Do you like busy crowded places or do you want to be far from them?

- Do you want custom designed small specialty tours with highly qualified local guides or are you ready to get on the bus with thirty others?

- Are you a gourmand or do you love Mickey D's?

As you can see, a traveller needs to give some thought to their travels, and most do. Make a Travel Advisor's job a little easier by providing as much information about your expectations as you can. While privacy is a concern, you should be as open as possible about the value you're looking for so there isn't too much guesswork involved. Rather than flog some wild guesses at a client, Advisors like to talk about your specific needs.

Are there deals or sales out there? All the time! Are they what you want and when you want them, and do they represent good value to you? There is a difference between a deal and something that is good value. I couldn't come close to guessing how many times I've had people come into our agency and ask "Are there any good sales/deals to be had?" There may be deals and sales but rarely are they good value, unless you think a Caribbean beach is a great place to be… during hurricane season.

5.
WHAT A TRAVEL ADVISOR KNOWS!

HAVE YOU ever visited a travel agency and asked them about a specific flight, package, or cruise you saw in an advertisement?

Do you know what the first thing most Advisors will say?

It's not what you might think. The first words out of their mouths will apt to be, ***"Let me see if there is any space."***

It's not about price or anything else. The first thing the Advisor needs to know is if what you want is available for the dates and/or times you want it. The Advisor is identifying the most important consideration in trying to make a booking. Is it available to meet your requirements?

The next biggest consideration is will it be available when it comes time to actually book and pay for it. It's not uncommon in our business to find that by the time a client decides to book, the space is no longer there. Many times I've had clients say that the 'product' is exactly what they want; they just need to check with their spouse/travelling companion and they'll get back to me. Then when they do, the product is sold out at the price shown in the ad. A couple of years ago I had a client come to me for prices for a direct flight from Toronto to Amsterdam in Air Transat's Club Class seats. I gave her the information and then didn't hear from the client for five weeks. I don't really need to tell you when she called back, the flight she wanted was sold out in Club Class.

This is frustrating to everyone.

The Advisor knows that travel products are limited in the amounts made available by the supplier, particularly during a sale. As an example, an airline will advertise that an airfare seat sale from Vancouver to Toronto is only $455.00.

What they don't say is that the seats are only available at unattractive departure times and, even then, there may be a very limited number of seats at the price advertised. A flight leaving at two p.m.and arriving at ten p.m. may only have two seats at the sale price, while the overnight 'Redeye' leaving at midnight has twenty-five seats at the advertised price. The same principle applies to things like cruises, coach tours, and even hotel rooms.

The other thing that some consumers can forget is that the only reason something is on sale is that the provider couldn't sell them at their full price and so they offer them at a discount to get rid of the last few seats. Normally this happens only close to the departure date. Today there are some amazingly well designed 'yield management' programs that tell suppliers how many seats/ rooms/cabins to sell at what price and when to sell them. These systems are dynamic and are updating their pricing by the hour in some cases. There are fewer last-minute rush seats on sale.

So, my advice to you when you're dealing with a Travel Advisor is to have them check not only the price but also the availability and the number of seats/packages/cabins left at that price so that you know if you're in a situation where there is limited capacity. It can reduce frustrations.

6.
WORKING WITH AN AGENCY

CONTRARY TO some opinions in the industry, I don't believe you need to have a Travel Advisor handle all of your travel activity. There are also times when you should use an Advisor regardless of the number of trips you've already done for yourself. There are other times when you can take care of your own arrangements. Following are a couple of lists of each for you to consider.

When to consider using an Advisor to help you arrange your travel:

- International airfares, particularly if they involve more than a simple round-trip ticket. Most people have no idea how complicated the rules for international air fares can be. This is especially so when more than one carrier is involved.

- The overall trip is complicated and complex involving multiple modes of transportation, special accommodations and critical timings that must be met.

- Multi-components and modes are involved. Trains and boats and planes wait for no one. An Advisor can help take the stress out of connections. See Chapter 11.

- You should use an agent any time the travel involves crossing a border where you need a travel visa/permit from the arrival country. It's an extreme possibility but nobody needs to risk time in jail because they don't have the correct documents for entering the country. These things change all the time.

- Get help if you're getting married overseas. If nothing else, the families involved will have someone else other than you to complain to about the arrangements. I speak from practical experience!

- If you have health complications to consider, an Advisor can help you ensure things go well. A simple thing like the wrong type of oxygen canister on an airplane can be a problem. The Advisor can also get you any information you need such as Government Advisories about care at the destinations you're visiting.

- New destinations to you. If nothing else, if you're going somewhere new, it helps to have someone, who, even if they've not been there, has had to solve problems for others they sent to the same destination. If they've been there and are a specialist on the destination, they are Ken Jennings to your Joe Schmuck!

- Travelling with children when you're not a custodial parent. They may be your nieces and nephews or your kids' best friends but you need to be aware that the various border authorities are very careful with people travelling with children who are not their own.

- Honeymoons. You want to start this part of your life together on the right foot. It's a stressful time, good stress, but still stressful and you want things to go right. Grooms are you listening?

- If you have a criminal record. Many countries don't welcome criminals, even fully reformed individuals who have a record - anywhere. Customs people all over the world have access to what you may think are sealed records. Police forces cooperate!

- As a general observation, if you're not a well-organized person, get help!

Here are some cases when you can do it yourself:

- Simple domestic air tickets. Round trip air from Toronto to Vancouver. If you're comfortable making the arrangements, go for it. However, remember if something goes wrong (weather/ health scares) you'll need to deal with the airline directly

- Car rental only. Other than having the wrong car, or being sold out when you arrive (it does happen, but not frequently), not much possibility of a problem.

- A road trip, if where you stop doesn't matter to you. You just pull over and get a room. Not much an Advisor can do for you here.

- Simple North American hotel bookings. Unless you're picky, then you might want someone with a little pull to help you get exactly the room you want, overlooking the ocean for example.

- A simple 'cruise only' booking in the Caribbean and you're driving to the departure port. What can happen to cause you a problem?

- If you've just committed murder, book the trip yourself, I don't want anything to do with you! Just for the record it happened at an agency I owned on the west coast. I hear it was eventually reduced to manslaughter. He never got his money back and we didn't get our commission!

- If you're transporting illegal drugs, again, we don't want anything to do with you. Been there, don't want to go again! We don't enjoy having to deal with the RCMP about your travel arrangements (on VIA Rail - no security or baggage checks!). They're pleasant but insistent people.

- When the 'deal' is more important to you than the travel. For us, travel is not a game, it is fun but it's not a game for us.

Many, if not most people just don't understand how Advisors can be useful to a traveller. If you're not sure, just ask a Travel Advisor.

7.
GOVERNMENT FORMALITIES

LIFE CAN get complicated at times. If you travel to points outside Canada it can be very complicated!

I won't get into detailed requirements here for specific destinations, but I do want you to understand that you need to be aware of where you're going and the rules and formalities that may apply to you.

Also, you'll need some idea of geography as it can offer some nasty surprises if you're not careful. For a crazy example, on a non-stop flight from Toronto to Vancouver most people don't realize that on many west-bound flights, much of the flight may happen physically over the USA. It's considered a domestic flight as there's no stop in any other country...unless the aircraft needs to make an unscheduled stop in Montana! It happens. The aircraft may develop a mechanical problem or a passenger may become sick, it could even be you. If you're in the middle of some personal disagreement with the US government then things may be about to get worse. If it's you who is sick, then I hope you have out of country medical insurance. It doesn't happen every day and the physical flight route can change day to day depending on weather and winds aloft. Having a passport with you and having an annual out of province medical policy are good ideas if you're doing something like this on a regular basis.

If you're going to travel outside Canada, then planning and preparation are extremely important. Universally, you'll need a passport for travel to other countries and for many you'll need some other more specific forms of authorization to enter the destination, such as a visa (not the credit card type!) or an ETA (Electronic Travel Authorization), both of which need to be in place before you depart. There are at least two places a Canadian can go to determine specific requirements. Here are the websites:

- Canadian Government:
  https://Travel.gc.ca/travelling/advisories

- IATA (International Air Transport Association):
  https://www.iata.travelcentre.com/

IATA is the international trade association for airlines. They want things to go well for you as they can end up paying heavy fines from the destination country if they carry someone into a country who doesn't have the correct documentation. They are also responsible for returning you to your origin, if you're not in jail.

A couple of other quick points. Some countries need your passport to be valid for at least three or six months beyond your expected departure date from the country. Look before you book!

Always carry the contact details of Canadian embassies or consulates in the countries you're visiting. You'll need those if you lose or have your passport stolen.

The Canadian government site also has a pretty comprehensive summary of security information needed by travellers. Take a look at the one for Mexico for example in the above-mentioned website. It'll scare the crap out of you!

As mentioned in the previous chapter, if you're travelling with children, especially if they are not your children, life has become much more complicated. Single custodial parents must be careful. I hope you have a notary on your speed dial, they'll make your life easier. Again, check the requirements of the specific country of your destination (and any stops in between) and check what the Canadian Border Service Agency (CBSA) is looking for when you return to the country. If your kids are underage, don't sign their Canadian passport for them, it will invalidate the document. Hopefully you won't run into an uninformed US border agent who doesn't realize this and forces you to sign on the child's behalf.

If you're off to exotic locales you'll also want to check the Canadian government website for health concerns and other medical requirements. You need to do this well in advance as some preparatory requirements must be met well before you leave; 'read' here, nasty needles!

Personally, importing items into Canada can be a funny business. Again, check out the site if you plan to bring back anything wild or wonderful or valuable.

Enjoy your travels but be aware of all of your responsibilities. Your Travel Advisor can help you by providing information but rarely can they do many of these things for you.

8.
UNDERSTANDING AIR TRAVEL

THIS IS almost an impossible chapter to write. For it to be of any practical day to day use, it would need to be as long as an encyclopedia! However, I'll try to provide an overview.

It helps to remember that the first powered, commercially-scheduled flight happened only about 116 years ago between St. Petersburg and Tampa, Florida and cost a passenger $5.00. In those days, the city of St. Petersburg gave the carrier a subsidy of $40 per day to operate the flights. Three months later the city cancelled the subsidy and the operation ceased. Well into the late 1970s and early 1980s, this model of subsidies and public convenience was the norm for many carriers, especially in the US and Canada. Then things were deregulated. It took a little longer in Canada to sort out, as is the norm. Now, pretty much throughout the free world, air carriers can write their own rules and set their own prices. However, I should point out that there is a bit of a trend for governments to insert themselves back into commercial regulations as airlines may have pushed things too far in their own favour.

The airline business is not like a city bus service. Almost all carriers today are normal commercial businesses with shareholders and management like any other company (although some nations still own or subsidize their national carriers, most of which are unsuccessful, see Alitalia!). They need to make a profit so the prices they charge are ringed by tariff rules that protect the shareholder's investment and insure they can continue as a going concern. Notice, I didn't say "protect their passenger".

As a passenger buying a ticket on a flight now, you don't really care about the details of how an airline works, you only want:

- To get safely to your destination.

- To be as comfortable as possible.

- To arrive as close to the time the airline promised.

- As low a price as is available.

You're not at all concerned with all the archaic airlines' rules and regulations when things go well. Honestly, to the vast number of the people using the system today or working in it, they don't care either. Until, that is, **things stop working** the way they are planned or should work.

When things do go wrong today, passengers want to know what the rules are, and what compensation they are due for the delays, injury, or inconveniences and lost property. You should be able to know or find details of the rules and laws that apply to their problems and find them easily. You'll have to look hard, as the regulators and air carriers don't make it simple to find these details, unless you know where to look.

It helps to understand to some small degree how the industry is structured if you're to understand the rules that apply. We'll start at the high level and work down.

At the international level there are two main bodies involved in regulating the operation of an airline.:

- International Civil Aviation Organization (ICAO) which is a special agency of the United Nations charged with setting the standards and rules for air navigation, safety, and aircraft technical operations other than the 'commercial' aspects of operating an airline. Its members are the nations of the world. Its headquarters are in Montreal. You shouldn't really need to worry about these people. If you want to get into more depth on this, check out Wikipedia. For most passengers this is at the esoteric end of things.

- International Air Transport Association (IATA) is the trade association of most of the world's airlines, again headquartered in Montreal. They set the commercial rules that apply to

structuring international fares and the rules associated with
each fare, especially if more than one airline is involved. Even
if the fare is specific to one airline, they tend to follow the same
format. Note, they don't set fares or publish them; they just set
what content should be in the rules, and generally how the rules
should be applied. Airlines themselves establish the fares and
the details of the rules, within the guidelines established by the
various governing bodies. The airlines are the characters you
want to watch closely!

Transport Canada is the Canadian national authority for both safety and commercial aspects of domestic and international services originating in Canada or within a Canadian jurisdiction. Again, they don't set the fares, although they can strongly encourage the airlines to fall in line, if they're so inclined. Sometimes they do get directly involved with how some rules should be applied. For example, how much you should get if you are delayed or bumped. That's because no one trusts the carriers to be fair or neutral. If it's about lost, damaged or delayed checked luggage there have been a good number of people in the news that have been particularly aggrieved. Ask anyone who checked their musical instrument as part of their luggage and had it returned with damage! Some have even written songs about their problems!

Now for the air carriers themselves. They are the ones that count when you get into problems. Carriers publish their fares themselves and through publishing companies for distribution to agents and websites in North America and around the world.

Let's take Air Canada as an example, as they operate domestically, in the transborder market, and internationally. Right at the bottom of the front page of their Canadian consumer website, in the last black bar, in very small print, underneath their copyright claim is a single digit pica point phrase you can click on that reads:

"General Conditions of Carriage & Tariffs"

Go ahead and click on it. You'll find another 300 or more pages of 'gobbly gook'. The first part is titled "Our Customer Commitment under the Canadian Air

Passenger Protection Regulations" which says a lot about lost luggage, delays or cancellations, denied boarding, seating children and additional Air Canada policies. If you think you might be interested, (i.e. if you've been delayed) here's where they say what they'll do to/for you. In the middle of that opening page you'll see a section called "Our Tariffs" where you can further click into details of their Domestic Tariff (89 pages), their International Tariff (116 pages), and a section called Carrier Surcharges (42 pages). THESE SECTIONS ARE WHERE SOME OF THE REAL MEAT IS HIDDEN. Next there's a whole section on Additional Air Canada Policies. Finally, you might get as far down in the rabbit hole as "Important Notices".

But wait! There's more!

Not only are the entire general rules applicable, but each international fare segment (i.e. for Montreal to London) has its own rule. Without going into the details there can easily be thirty different elements to each fare segment. Just as an example, here is a partial list of some of the more common terms addressed in the fare rules:

- General Description of the Fare

- Day & Time Restrictions

- Seasonal Restrictions

- Flight Restrictions

- Advance Reservation & Ticketing

- Minimum Stay Requirements

- Maximum Stay Requirements

- Stopover Restrictions

- Transfer Restrictions

- Combinability with Other Fares

- Surcharges

- Sales Restrictions

- Penalties

- Higher Intermediate Point (HIP) Exceptions (a real doozy of an obscure rule)

- Endorsements

- Discounts

- Tour Discounts

- Agent Discounts

- Voluntary Changes

- Voluntary Cancellations.

That lists just some of the more key elements involved with fare rules and they can run over ten pages. If any one of these factors change, the price may be changed by the airline.

Particularly with international flights, and especially where Air Canada (or any other airline) is cooperating with another carrier on one ticket, (i.e. Air Canada to London UK, then British Airways to Naples after a three day stop in London, then home to Canada on Alitalia a few days later) there may be three separate *fares* involved with three separate sets of rules and only the airlines (only sometimes!) know what rules apply if something goes wrong! For instance, say your guitar is damaged, who's responsible? Without help you don't stand a chance as they'll all try blaming one of the other carriers involved.

There are people who work for airlines and travel agencies who spend their whole working lives writing and interpreting these rules to ensure that the interests of the air carriers are protected!

Many, perhaps more accurately, most people who book their own travel don't know what they agree to when they check off on the Terms and Conditions they find on a website. It doesn't matter until something goes wrong.

Some travel agents are really good at this stuff. Some just want to book a simple cruise. Pick the right one when it comes to complicated air itineraries.

9.
A TRADE SECRET

FOR MUCH of what you see about air fares in the travel pages or the internet it's 'what you see is what you get'. However, when it comes to many international air fares, there are some things that are hidden from most travellers.

Airline pricing ranks right up there with nuclear physics when you want to talk about complex subjects, so here is a very much simplified version of what happens.

International airlines cooperate on a lot of aspects of travel. They are members of alliances. They sell connecting flights on other carriers; they have arrangements where other carriers do their airport handling or they will switch cargo to another carrier if they're short of space in their holds. At times they may even ask other carriers to operate their flights for them. Yet they do compete on price. One thing they don't like doing is sharing information with other carriers about their lowest and most competitive prices. They don't want to be undercut or be forced into a price war.

One of the ways they make their lowest fares opaque to their competitors is to only offer it as an unpublished fare through 'wholesaler' style travel agencies. They are sometimes referred to as Consolidators in the industry. In essence, Consolidators sign contracts with specific airlines where they receive a volume discount for selling a set dollar value of that airline's tickets. For example, Air Portugal may offer 'XYZ' agency (who specializes in travel to Portugal) a 25% discount on their lowest public fare if 'XYZ' sells a minimum of $5 million in tickets that year. It ensures that a little-known airline can fill its aircraft on a thin or seasonal route. 'XYZ' then may offer these special prices to other agencies (who are not big sellers of Portugal) or their own clients as part of a land package. This happens on many highly popular leisure travel routes.

Some Consolidators do so much business that they don't sell to the general public at all, as it's too much of a problem for them; they only sell to other agencies. In all cases, the prices can come out lower than the lowest published public fares and everybody makes a good margin on the deal. This is how many of the high-volume website agencies work. Need to know more? Ask your Travel Advisor.

Many of these unpublished fares usually have severe restrictions on changes, cancellations, frequent flyer miles accumulations and so forth. They may also be very specific flights, specific seasons, and usually don't allow them to be combined with other fares for complicated routes. These fares can also appear when an airline does not fly directly between two points but forces you to connect in their main hub, such as a Toronto-Stockholm flight connecting via Helsinki. In this case, Finnair may offer a pretty good discount for accepting the inconvenience and extra time the connecting flights require.

Sometimes these fares are even offered on business class seats. KLM did this at one time, offering a fare of approximately CAD $3,800 for a ticket that would normally set you back about $8,000! It's still expensive, but cheaper than walking up to the ticket counter a couple of hours before the flight and buying full fare. In most cases you'll need to ask your Travel Advisor if they sell this type of ticket. Many do.

10.
CHEAP SEATS

THE IDEA of a really low, low, low price for a flight is intriguing. Some airlines use this 'low price' marketing tactic to lure passengers to their services, and it works. Most of the time!

We tend to refer to these types of carriers as low cost/budget/discount/no frills or a regional carrier. Personally, I'm a bit ambivalent about them. When they're good they can be just the right solution to a travel problem. I have been on a couple of these carriers and they were fine for me at the time. At other times, they may be a real horror show.

Scoring a cheap flight can leave a lot of money in a traveller's pocket to spend on something else. However, cheap prices aren't *always* a good thing.

First though, some of the positives:

- You only pay for what you need. If you don't care where you sit, or are not concerned about how early in the day you need to be at the airport or arriving at your destination in the middle of the night, they are fine.

- You can book these online, yourself. No need to use a travel professional if you don't want to.

There are some other things you need to consider that are neither bad nor good; you just need to be aware:

- While there are meals and refreshments on many of them, they're not free, and they may go for restaurant prices.

- You usually can't connect to a flight to an ultimate destination. Normally you would need two separate tickets and reservations and they treat any misconnect problems as yours, not theirs!

- Some (Ryanair for example), charge extra to use a credit card to pay for the flight.

- They charge extra for everything, checked baggage, your second carry-on item, seat assignment, and check-in at the airport.

Most don't work with travel professionals so if you do like to work with an Advisor, this can cause problems.

Some other observations:

- They don't work with other airlines, so if they oversell their own flight, they may not put you on another carrier even if there are no more of their own flights that day.

- Many don't sell connecting flights, even on their own service.

- Many fly only to secondary airports. As a prime example, the airport Ryanair uses for Paris, Beauvais, is anywhere from a 75 to 100 minute ground transfer from central Paris and costs about CAD $25 per person, each way.

- They have a habit of going out of business with little advance notice. I have a list of eighty-seven different budget carriers that closed down in the last few years. See WOW Air, Thomas Cook, Air Berlin, Canada 3000, Jetsgo and others.

So, what makes them so different that they can sell their services cheaper than traditional airlines?

- They tend to fly one type of aircraft; i.e. Southwest and Ryanair both only fly Boeing 737 variants. This allows for simple pilot and mechanic training and efficient maintenance operations with fewer spare parts in inventory.

- Very few fly long haul flights and those that do, aren't normally successful.

- They fly to many secondary airports that charge less for landing and other rents and fees.

- They don't offer connections or interline services so as to keep their planes in the air more, where they make money. Most have to do five or more hops a day to provide a payoff for their shareholders.

- Almost all of them only sell tickets online. You don't see much TV advertising for these guys.

How are they the same as larger carriers?

- They pay approximately the same price for their aircraft as other airlines of the same size.

- They have pretty much the same price for fuel as other carriers buying the same volume of fuel.

- On the aircraft they have to have the same minimum number of employees as the big guys.

- They pay the same landing fees at airports as other carriers using the same aircraft.

So how do they keep their costs down so they can make money?

- Their labour costs tend to be lower than normal carriers as they pay somewhat less and many don't have a large number of long term unionized employees.

- They don't have some of the marketing and sales costs that larger carriers may have.

- They rely on their website to answer many questions, instead of people.

Over time these operators have been blamed by some for the rise of over-tourism at some destinations and are accused of having added to climate concerns due to their quick growth and diversion of passengers from trains to planes.

If you want to save money on routes where these companies fly, I recommend you stick to well-known brands that have operated successfully for a number of years. Here's a list of some of the world's biggest low-cost carriers who've been around for a few years:

- Southwest Airlines in the US.

- Ryanair in Europe.

- Easy Jet in Europe.

- Air Asia in Malaysia for Pacific area.

- Lion Air in the Philippines.

- JetBlue in the US.

- Vueling in Europe (sub of British Airways).

- Pegasus in Turkey.

11.
YOU CAN'T GET THERE FROM HERE!

YOU MAY have noticed that there aren't as many direct international flights to secondary airports on major carriers as there used to be. You often need to connect with another carrier to get to your destination. It seems that for many of the destinations you travel to these days, you need to connect at least once at some mid-point. This can also be expensive on major airlines so people look for low cost connections, usually on another airline using a separate ticket.

When you do connect, you have to allow a minimum amount of time to ensure you make the connection. Not surprisingly, airlines refer to this as the 'minimum connect time'. These are published in the airlines' tariffs (my bet is less than 1% of all passengers have seen one of these documents) and can be quite complicated.

There are many factors to be considered:

- Is the flight a domestic to domestic service?
- Is it an international flight connecting to a domestic flight?
- Is there a change of terminals, and so forth?
- What about baggage handling?
- Are customs or security involved?

There are just too many variables. When you book directly with an airline or a travel agent, their systems won't allow them to book a connecting flight on a through ticket that doesn't meet their minimum connect time as a matter of routine. However, if you book two separate flights on your own - you're on your own!

As an example, if you were looking for the least expensive route to Italy you might book a flight to London, England on Air Transat, then book a separate flight, on a separate ticket, from London to Pisa on Ryanair. It may save you money, especially if more than one person is travelling. It is your responsibility to allow enough time to make the connection. If you miss the second flight because you were delayed on your first flight, you are out of luck. Ryanair (or any other airline) will take the position that you 'no showed' through no fault of theirs (they can't know you're on an inbound international flight) and that they have no responsibility for you missing your flight and Ryanair will require you to buy another (normally much higher priced) ticket and give you no credit for the ticket you didn't use. As a result, this can be an expensive problem.

Using the same example, just how much time would you need? Let's take a look, working backward on what admittedly is a simple example, but not an unrealistic one:

- Check-in time needed for Ryanair at Stansted Airport north of London = 1.5 to 2 hours

- Train from London Liverpool station to Stanstead Airport = 1 hour

- Subway from Victoria Station to Liverpool Station = 20 minutes

- Gatwick Airport to London Victoria Station = 30 minutes

- Arrival formalities at Gatwick Airport (customs, luggage recovery, etc.) = 1.5 hours

- Allowance for late arrival due to poor weather, ATC delays, delayed departure = 1 hour

Total time needed, approximately 6.5 hours. A reasonable time allowance for the connection would be a minimum seven to eight hours, so if your flight to Pisa was to leave London at four p.m. London time you should plan to arrive in London no later than ten a.m. and eight a.m. would be better! It might save you a bit of money over using British Airways or Alitalia on a through ticket, but is a loss of 6.5 hours in transfers worth it when you only have a week of holidays?

I don't know about you, but if I'm on a holiday, I don't need that type of stress. Some people are pretty good at making their way through airports. Others want to be relaxed! Be careful! If you're in a hurry, it may end up costing you more than you thought.

12.
WHAT DOES "FQTV" MEAN ON MY AIR CANADA BOARDING PASS?

THAT'S SIMPLE. The FQTV (followed by a number) is there to indicate that the appropriate miles/points in Air Canada's frequent flyer program/reward program, Aeroplan, have been credited to your account. If you used a Travel Advisor, they input that number in the PNR (Passenger Name Record)* they created to book your flight (if you gave it to them) to ensure that you get proper credit on your account. With Air Canada, anybody can accumulate points by either using a sponsoring credit card or actually flying some miles, or by both.

Air Canada uses Aeroplan to encourage real frequent flyers to earn special status depending on the miles they've physically flown, the flight segments they've flown, or the dollars they've spent on tickets. For this, they get special treatment for things like seat assignments, discounts, wait listing, check-in and so forth. They plan to merge it all, perhaps due to the present confusion and unnecessary complications. Watch for announcements when they figure it out. I'm not holding my breath.

While an agent can add your frequent flyer number to any booking they make for you, not many airlines allow an Advisor to make a reward booking on your behalf.

Frequent flyer programs were created decades ago (first by American Airlines) to give customers an incentive to stay loyal to one particular airline. Since then they've grown beyond all recognition. They've also lost much of their allure to leisure travellers as it is difficult to accumulate enough points to book anything. Today, it's easier to accumulate Aeroplan points using a credit card loyalty benefit than it is to book something based on your flying activity, unless you travel frequently for business.

Aeroplan is different than the blue carded Air Miles offered by Loyalty One companies. That's a program for non-frequent flyers allowing them to get rewards such as flights or 'stuff' for money spent in various retail sponsors.

The real challenge for a Travel Advisor with these point products is when a couple comes in wanting to book two flights on a matching itinerary; one using a points balance and the other buying a ticket. When this happens, the best thing to do is gamble, do a little research then book the frequent flyer ticket first. Once that's confirmed, buy a revenue ticket for the other person. It will probably cost you more than you would otherwise pay, but at least they'll be on the same flights; if nothing changes!

As a user and collector of miles/points you'll need to understand the rules of any plan you use, as there can be ugly surprises. FYI, on Air Canada, at the time of writing, if there hasn't been any activity (collecting or using of miles) in a specified period (a year currently), you may find the airline has cancelled <u>all</u> of your points. Suddenly your balance is zero. This recently happened to somebody with a Canadian airline and the collector only got them returned after they howled loudly in the press. Be warned.

- * *"Passenger Name Record" is the computer reservation system reference for a specific trip.*

13.
QUICK POINTS ABOUT BAGGAGE

THERE'S NOT much a Travel Advisor can do about baggage except inform you about various carriers' allowances and charges. Most people worry about air carrier limits for carry on and checked luggage. In many cases it will depend on the ticket you buy, with some airlines offering a high allowance (both in weight and total dimensions) for high paying passengers and less so for cheap seats.

Think about the following:

- Two-wheeled bags are better than four-wheeled ones for a couple of reasons. First, airlines have dimensional limits for checked luggage and a bag with four wheels can waste space as the wheels are usually attached to the exterior and take up space. A two wheeled bag can have the wheels built into the body of the bag so you should end up with a larger capacity inside. Four wheels are not too bad on an airports' smooth marble floor but try wheeling a four-wheel bag along the cobbled streets of Italy. Been there, tried that, didn't work!

- Never put high value stuff in a checked bag. They can legitimately be opened by security people and illegitimately by others. You've been warned!

- Always attach your name and contact details to the exterior of any piece of luggage, and not with a little note held there with scotch tape. Use a proper bag tag. Even better, put your full contact information inside the bag as bag tags can become unglued!

- If you can, before your luggage disappears down the conveyor belt, and you know the code for your destination, make sure your bag is tagged correctly for its final destination by airport code, not just city code. Go online and search for IATA airport codes. Note that some cities (i.e. London) can have as many as five different airports! For London they are LHR, LGW, STN, LTN, and LCY. (Heathrow/Gatwick/Stansted/Luton/City). Be prepared to pay a fee for checked bags at the airport, especially so with discount carriers. Sometimes it can be even more than what you paid for your ticket!

- If you're a couple, each of you should carry a bit of the other person's wardrobe in your bags. If one of your or their bags goes 'walkabout', you at least have a change of clothes for your partner, until their bag shows up.

- Buy colourful bags. Today most are black, grey or other dark colours. It's hard to see your bag if it looks like everybody else's coming down the conveyor belt. It also ensures someone else doesn't mistake your bag for theirs and walks off with it by mistake.

- FYI, if you buy an Air Canada ticket on a code-share flight physically operated by United Airlines, it's the United Airlines baggage rules that apply.

Hope this helps the next time you fly. Not much else an Advisor can do but help you avoid making a mistake.

14.
SEASONAL HEADS-UP

FLYING IS pretty routine now-a-days. However, weather always plays a role in aviation, and many times it rules. Other than when the air is turbulent, cruising along at 35,000 feet or so is normally pretty uneventfull, on a well-planned flight. The operative word here is well-planned. Before the aircraft even leaves the ground, a lot of time and experience goes into understanding the weather and working out a flight plan that minimizes the weather's effect on the flight. Where weather is of most concern is during the departure and arrival phases. In these phases of a flight, slow speeds, proximity to the ground, and other departing and arriving traffic all are part of the consideration. An icy runway (or an icy aircraft wing) can cause big delays for any flight. Mother nature can be fickle. How many times have passengers been told that their flight has been delayed because of weather, yet they look outside and it's beautiful and sunny and have a clear view for miles? Don't forget it might not be the same at your destination thousands of miles away or where your aircraft is starting its day.

As a passenger, there are a few things you can do that may help you improve the odds on reaching your destination on time:

- If possible, catch the first flight of the day. The aircraft you'll be on probably arrived the night before. If the weather is cruddy you don't have to worry if your inbound aircraft will arrive on time, all things being equal. Most aircraft operated by major carriers fly five or six legs a day. If weather is bad, they can get way behind.

- Try not to take flights that involve connections, especially in places that experience real winter. A couple of years ago my barber and his family had to take three different flights home from a cruise. (I didn't book them)! After two or three schedule changes and missed connections, they made it as far as Philadelphia at which point the carrier said, "Sorry, the next earliest flight we have for you is the day after tomorrow." The cost of renting a van to drive home a day late more than offset the money they saved by taking a cheap flight with two connections in each direction.

- Try not to check any bags as they can be a casualty of the bad weather or a heavy load of expedited cargo, especially around Christmas. Also, if you must connect or change aircraft, you have a better chance if you and the gate agent aren't worried about luggage.

- Call ahead. Check your flight well in advance. Go online or call the carrier and make sure things are working normally. If there are problems building up it may help you to adjust your plans. It's no fun if your family members are waiting at the destination not knowing your schedule has changed and you're going to be six hours late.

- It isn't only winter that can be a problem. Atlantic storms can make it difficult to get into places like Miami for a cruise.

- High winds on the island of Madeira can make a landing feel like a monster roller coaster ride. See **https://www.youtube. com/watch?v=9KLwX01I-3o**.

- Beautiful clear day but windy? A recent such storm in the UK with 30 to 45 knot winds really made landings difficult in the Midlands. Some flights had to divert to airports all around England.

- On a clear but really hot day at a high altitude airport, like La Paz in Bolivia (13,323 feet above sea level) and if the winds are in the wrong direction, the pilot may need to keep a number of seats empty to just get off the ground even with a 4,000 metre runway. Places like that, you need to check in early.

- Europe with its fog can be difficult. I was once on a flight into Amsterdam when we couldn't see the ground even after we landed. This definitely slows things down.

- The result: Mother Nature-1, Airline-0! Mother Nature always wins. If you're travelling, watch the weather.

15.
SLOW TRAVEL

EVERYBODY HAS a 'travel style'. A travel style is the cumulative result of the way in which you travel. There are many styles. For example, people can be peripatetic travellers; they can be tourists; they can be experiential vacationers and then there are the slow travellers. Each person travels in the way that is of interest and comfortable to them.

The slow traveller approach is an off shoot of the slow movement which in turn produced the slow food movement. These are people who want to get away from fast food and who enjoy the time needed to prepare and eat a meal made from ingredients native to their locale. Slow travelling is a state of mind that values the intensity of time spent in engaging the people they meet in their wandering. To them the local people are as important as the sights and sounds of the monuments and attractions that get a destination into a guide book.

Here are some of the ideas that are key for a slow traveller:

- Slow travellers prefer to walk, use bicycles, local trains and buses, boats and ferries in contrast to airplanes and high-speed trains.

- Slow travellers spend time checking out local stores and markets to take advantage of the opportunity to meet people.

- Slow travellers don't let speed and anticipation of their destination eclipse the joy of the journey.

- Slow travellers spend time sitting around a local café and doing some serious people watching. Sorry Starbucks!

- A slow traveller stays in one place for more than a day or so. Typically, they hang around for a week or two in a short-term rental.

- Slow travellers take the time to pick up a little of the local language and try buying a local newspaper and work their way through it to find out what is of interest to people in their destination.

- If they can't stay for a week or so, a slow traveller stays in locally owned and operated hotels, guest houses, B & B's and inns giving themselves the opportunity to meet the locals.

- They eat locally at restaurants that don't post their menu in English; it's just in the local language.

- Slow travellers enjoy the unexpected. Delays and cancellations create new opportunities to mingle with the locals.

- Slow travellers go beyond what is in a guide book. They get involved in what the locals do.

While many of us can't follow all of these precepts on all of our travels, we can mix some of these ideas into our own travels so that we enrich our own travel experience.

16.
GEEZER TRAVEL

WELCOME TO my world. Many of us look forward to retirement as it gives us the time and flexibility to travel. Of course for many, it is also a time of decreased income and the worry about making the best use of the funds we have for our travel plans. Here are a few ideas of ways to get the most use of your travel dollars without compromising on your experiences.

Look at alternative forms of accommodations. For most, the price of where we stay when we're on the road can be the single largest travel cost we'll have to cover. Besides hotels, you can arrange accommodations in short term rentals such as apartments in Paris or farm houses in Tuscany; even house exchanges and house sitting in many destinations will reduce costs. Also, alternative accommodations can help keep other costs, particularly meals under control. Three restaurant meals a day can drain the pocket book quickly.

Most retirees have friends who also like to travel. Travel with your friends and share costs such as car rentals and accommodations. It can have a significant impact. Even if you plan to be away for three or four weeks, sharing a place for a week or two when you meet up with friends will help.

Sometimes the longer you stay the less your costs on a per day basis may be. While renting a place in Italy for a week might cost CAD $800, the same place for a month may only be $2,400, particularly if it isn't high season. Also, the longer you stay away the better the possibility of renting out your own place at home for the duration. Think house exchanges.

Travel when others aren't. It's no secret that it costs less to travel in low and shoulder seasons than in high season.

Look around and find a good quality out of country travel medical insurance policy if you're not covered as part of your retirement benefits. Shop around. This is not something to go cheap on. Make sure the policy covers your individual situation. Also plan your regular medical requirements around your travel schedule if you can, so you don't need to come home for something you could change without concern.

As a retiree plan your more strenuous destination visits before you get too old to do it reasonably. In my practice I didn't see too many people head to Africa after they reached their mid 70s. People are staying healthy much longer these days, but don't bet your bucket list on it!

Be flexible. Be ready when a good deal appears to a place you've always wanted to see. The costs can be discounted up to 50% in some cases, again particularly so at the beginning and end of the 'season' of a particular destination.

17.
BE CAREFUL OUT THERE!

WHAT DO all of the following stories have in common?

- Your friend has a heart attack while the two of you are walking the trail between Vernazza and Monterosso in the Cinque Terre. The vacation is over and the two of you need to head home early. The doctor says she can travel home for further treatment.

- You and your wife are crossing the street two days prior to your vacation when a driver runs a red light and breaks your leg. At least he waited around for the police and ambulance.

- You and your three girl friends are enjoying a week away in a five star resort in Puerto Vallarta when you get a call from a nice young policeman saying your husband has just passed away.

- Natalie, your young daughter has suddenly been hospitalized at home. Her grandmother (and baby sitter) called you in Varadero, Cuba to bring you up to date.

- Your girlfriend (who is a landed immigrant from Romania, not a Canadian citizen) comes home from the US Consulate and tells you that they have refused to give her a visa to transit LA airport on the way to your fully prepaid dream vacation in Bora Bora.

- You're forced to cancel a Mediterranean cruise because you've been called for jury duty.

What do all these incidents have in common? They are all situations that my clients have faced in the last fifteen years or so. In all cases not only was there financial loss, there was the need to help in making arrangements and communicating with others to let them know what was happening.

Each of these clients (except one) had travel/medical plus cancellation and trip interruption insurance, so their monetary losses were covered and they had the help of the insurance company. For many people, the money they spend on their vacation is the 3rd largest expenditure they make after homes and cars. A cancelled trip can easily cost $5,000 to $10,000 and for most of us, that's real money.

For Canadians and especially Ontarians who travel out of the country, private emergency medical insurance coverage is a necessity. You can't count on your provincial health plan to pick up your medical expenses when you travel, or even part of it like you used to be able to do. As an example, as of 2020, Ontario's Health Plan provided a maximum payment of CAD $0.00 per day for outpatient emergency room services. If it is inpatient hospital services, the coverage maximum payment the Plan would make is CAD $0.00. If needed, Ontario's Health Plan will pay CAD $0.00 per day for operating room costs, coronary care units, intensive care, neonatal or pediatric special care unit services. At the beginning of 2020, the government of the province eliminated all out of country coverage through the provincial plan. A huge outcry reversed this somewhat, but you need to check what your province will pay.

This means you need to purchase out of province medical/travel insurance. However, there are a few things you should know when you start looking around for a provider.

- All travel medical insurance policies are not the same. Take a look at a minimum of at least three different policies. Find the best one for you. Each separate insurance underwriter sells their own individual policy that is worded to their way of thinking, so you can't just assume they are all the same. Remember, they're in the business to make money!

- Check out the online reviews of the insurers you're thinking of doing business with. When you're buying an insurance policy, you're buying a promise by the insurer that they'll pay your medical bills if something goes wrong while you're out of the province. You really want to know how well the insurer keeps their promise. While somewhat regulated, some are better at keeping their promises than others. The real cost to you is not the premium you pay for the coverage; it's what you might be faced with if your insurer won't pay. Don't go for the lowest premium. Go for the one with the best reputation!

- Read the damned policy before you buy it! Read it critically. What does it say, even more important what doesn't it say? WARNING: This can be dull and hard work. Watch for weasel words and phrases. My favourite is *"reasonable and customary charges."* This should be interpreted to mean "as little as we can get away with paying, prove otherwise." Ask pointed questions and note the person you talked with and the date and time. They can't change the policy and they're not allowed to lie to you. Don't assume anything.

- If you're of a certain age, you'll need to complete a medical questionnaire before the underwriter will write a policy and give you a price for the coverage. You need to be very careful that you answer the questions correctly. There's not much room to fudge or make honest mistakes. When you apply for travel medical insurance you're contractually giving the insurer the right to question your personal physician(s) and see your files. A mistake here can and will void the policy. "Your travel agent is not permitted to help you fill out the questionnaire." ... is on the cover page of one of Canada's major insurers' questionnaire in a big red stop sign. You're on your own here! If you have questions, talk to your doctor.

- The same rules may apply to policies that are included in a credit card or provided by your employer. I can't tell you how many times people have told me that they are covered at work or by their credit card. Fine, but read the policy! Don't assume. They can be more or less restrictive and they can be limited in duration or coverage. Read the policy. Many people can't even find their copy of their employers' coverage or they threw out

the extra 'bumph' that came with their credit card and they
don't bring it with them when they travel and might need to call
on the coverage.

For all my cynicism, I still think you're outright irresponsible if you leave home without it. Travel medical insurance is a subject that too few people give much vigorous thought to before they travel. With all the sensational horror stories in the broadcast media lately it's important to do quality homework before you go.

There are two generic types of travel insurance: **Travel Medical Insurance** or **Trip Interruption and Cancellation Insurance**. There are packages that combine these and some other minor benefits. Honestly, you're crazy to leave home without some sort of coverage.

18.
MAKING YOUR OWN
HOTEL BOOKINGS

WHILE I'M a huge fan of using a Travel Advisor, sometimes it's not worth it just to book a hotel room, more so if the Advisor doesn't know the destination. When you do it yourself, here are a couple of things to consider.

There are numerous resources you can use to get information on hotels, their locations and pricing. Online sites like Booking.com and Expedia.com and many others offer deals on hotels. Yet most of the time, I'm not sure they are the best place to book. There are so many factors to consider. For some stays, the location is a key concern. In Rome for example, you don't want to be out in the outskirts if you want to spend your active time in the ancient city. Sometimes low cost is your driving force. Sometimes the hotel is in a resort type of location and you want specifically to be there. Each stop on an itinerary will have its own critical criteria. By all means look at the big sites but realize that once you have a specific property you might be interested in, there is one site you should always check before you book.

Go look at your target hotels' own website.

You need to remember that the hotel will be paying somewhere between 10% and 20% or more to a booking engine for any booking you make through the megasite booking engine. Several of the big sites even offer some travel agents a commission on the price you see through 'trade only' versions of the booking engines site. While the owner can make a higher margin if they take a booking directly from the traveller, if they are so inclined, there is another problem. The prices they offer on their own website will seldom undercut the price the megasites offer. A hotelier needs to keep the big sites sweet as they are the source of a high percentage of their bookings. So, don't book at the hotel's own site either.

Make your inquiry directly with the hotel via old fashion email. At this point, the transaction will become opaque to others, in most cases. So, the hotelier is free to offer any price they want to offer, or add into your booking extra amenities at little or no cost. Instead of paying for breakfast, maybe they make it part of the booking. It doesn't always work but it's worth the try.

When you send the email, be specific. The email should have your complete contact info, the number of people in the party, the bedding configuration, the date and time you will check in and the date and time of check out. Even mention the pricing you saw on a megasite and then ask for a better deal! Also consider asking about the terms and conditions attached to their direct rate, things such as refundability or changes.

This approach works well with European hotels but there is one thing you should do. When you've composed your email, cut and paste it into something like Google's translation app and put both the English and the translated version in the email you send. Most of the time when you send this off, there's a good chance that the person reading it at the other end will not have English as their first language. This is especially so when the email arrives at night when some young inexperienced front desk individual may be dealing with overnight inquiries. The consideration you show by doing this may put the person receiving your email in a considerate mood. Also, it may help you get an answer (in the hoteliers' language) in a more timely way than a request in English only might get. You can also use this approach to get help on many other things like airport pickup, prearranged attraction tickets and so forth. Having the hotel know who you are and what a considerate person you are, may be just the incentive they need to go above and beyond their 'ordinary'. It doesn't work all the time but many times it does. Many locally owned European hotels tend to be small/medium size family operations. They like to deal with real people.

Good luck!

19.
IS A VILLA RENTAL FOR YOU?

DID YOUR family ever have or rent a cottage for part of a summer vacation when you were a kid? It's almost a rite of passage for a Canadian and it's a great and inexpensive way to see a part of the countryside. Renting a 'villa' in Italy, France, or any other destination is a riff on the same theme you could consider for your next trip to Europe or beyond. It can be a great and relatively inexpensive way to see the countryside or a city. It's a chance to see how the locals live. An apartment in Rome or Paris is similar but urban oriented. This was happening long before Airbnb came along. Cottages or castles, apartments, town or country, farm vacations, winery vacation rentals, agriturismo, holiday homes or villas are all part of one of the more enriching ways of putting a temporary roof over your head while experiencing Europe.

We've rented seven or eight different places in Europe on our various trips over the years and enjoyed almost every one of them. We've also arranged for many of our clients to do the same and invariably they've also enjoyed their time. This is a particularly good approach for large family get-to-gathers and wedding parties.

To do it successfully there are a number of factors you need to consider:

- When and how long will you need it? It'll be no surprise if I tell you that summer is the most popular time of the year. However, unlike some Canadian camps or cottages, many places can be used year-round. High season is the most expensive time and the most sought-after period. Need I say that the best ones are reserved months and in some cases years in advance? While many can be rented for shorter periods, most want you to take the place for at least a week at a time in the high season. The vast majority work on a Saturday to Saturday basis.

- Be aware that in Italy most stores and shops in small towns are closed on Sundays. So if your vacation rental is like most in high season, renting on a Saturday to Saturday basis, make sure to allow time for grocery shopping on Saturday after arrival if you plan to eat at your vacation property on Sunday.

- Location is important. City or country? If it's to be in Tuscany for example you'll need to give some thought to where in this region you want to spend your time: south of Siena, around Florence, over near Lucca or close to Cortona. The same applies to France: down near the Cote D'Azur, in the Luberon hills, Burgundy, or the Loire Valley? I know; too many choices.

- What style of property do you want to use? Stand-alone house, vacation apartment, or castle? The type of accommodation will depend on your preference and budget. Resort complexes have a large number of apartments that are great if you have kids who want to hang out with other kids, at least part of the time. We once arranged a fifteen bedroom, true villa for a large extended family having a reunion.

- Do you need to be close to services like shopping, restaurants, and coffee houses or do you want to be away from it all for a little time of your own?

- Bedrooms and Baths: You need to decide. We often travelled with other couples and normally we wanted a separate bedroom and bath for each couple. With large families it can be a little cozier. You do need to respect the landlord's number maximums, otherwise they may be breaking local fire and safety regulations.

- What do you want in exterior facilities? Do you need a pool? What about a BBQ or fire pit? Close to town or in the woods near hiking trails, bike routes or such?

- What other special things do you need in things like kitchens and dining facilities? Are you a gourmet cook or will you just be doing breakfasts at the villa and eating out each evening?

- What other special requirements are there for your accommodations? Are you smokers? Do you want laundry facilities? What about AC? Will there be disabled people in your party?

- What's your budget? I've seen places (apartments) around $500 per week to multiples of $10,000 per week.

- Do you understand the commercial aspects of the rental? Monies may be non-refundable. The landlord may want progressive payments. Do you know what needs to be paid locally, such as electrical usage, cleaning fees and others?

Vacation rentals offer many advantages over hotels, if you're ready to do your own thing.

Remember though, you're not in Kansas anymore! Things will and should be different, but that's part of the adventure and the fun of travelling to a new place.

20.
DIFFERENT STROKES FOR DIFFERENT FOLKS

IN A newspaper article a while back, Arthur Frommer, one of the grand old men of travel, lamented that cruise ships weren't like they used to be.

Arthur had been on a travel writers 'FAM' trip on the relatively new **Norwegian Epic** (capacity 4,100 people) and to quote him "…it was the worst recreational event of his life". He said the ship was noisy, jangled and hectic. He went on to say there was not a single quiet spot he could find for mere relaxation. When Arthur was growing up, the cruise industry was a collection of small exclusive ships that catered to moneyed individuals whose idea of excitement was to sit down with a good book in a deck lounger with a nice warm blanket wrapped around their legs. However, like me, Arthur is getting old and I'm afraid that time may be passing us both by.

The cruise industry wanted and needed to grow and prosper. One way to achieve this was to make the cruise experience available to more people at a price they could afford. Unit costs were reduced over the last three decades by making ships bigger and capable of carrying more passengers. Those new passengers wanted more to do onboard and the cruise industry was more than happy to accommodate them, for a price. Now some cruise ships feature loud contemporary music, big crowds of merry makers and too many middle-aged men waiting to go down a water slide with nary a library in sight. Some people want party boats, some people want the whole family to go on a cruise together, and others want fun and adventure ashore every day. Not everyone wants to do the same things on a cruise that Arthur or I might like to do.

His problem was that he was on the wrong ship! He wanted something quiet and traditional and he got a theme park of a cruise ship.

What Arthur knows, but failed to mention was that the industry offers many different types of on-board experiences. There is no reason why someone who wants to take a cruise shouldn't find the right cruise for them regardless of their age or interests. Ask a Travel Advisor who specializes in cruising. There are numerous different cruise lines with an equal variety of cruise experiences. Here's a list of just a few that come to mind:

- Princess Cruises
- Holland America
- Carnival Cruise Lines
- Celebrity Cruise
- Royal Caribbean International
- Norwegian Cruise Lines
- AIDA Cruises
- American Cruise Lines
- Azamara Club Cruises
- Birka Cruises
- Costa Cruises
- Cruise & Maritime Voyages
- Crystal Cruise
- Cunard Cruises
- Disney Cruise Lines
- Fred Olsen Cruise Lines
- Hapag-Lloyd Cruises
- Hurtigruten
- MSC Cruises
- Oceania Cruises
- P&O Cruises

- Phoenix Reisen

- Pullmantur Cruises

- Regent Seven Seas Cruises

- Seabourn Cruise Lines

- Silverseas Cruises

- Star Cruises

- Thomson Cruises

- Transocean Tours

- TUI Cruises

- Windstar Cruises.

This is only a partial list and doesn't even start to touch on river cruising. If you're having a difficult time trying to determine which one would work for you, there are just two things you need to do. First, determine what style of cruise experience you want, then talk to a knowledgeable Travel Advisor who can point you in the right direction to ensure you get what you really want.

21.
TIRED OF WAITING IN LINE?

I HAD a client return from a thirty-day holiday in Rome, Sorrento and Venice and she and her friend had a fabulous time. They're already talking about the next time. Over a couple of different conversations (each over an hour), they kept up a constant refrain about how they enjoyed Italy. There was only one problem they encountered that put them off. Although they had bought 'Skip the Lineup' passes for the Vatican Museum and Sistine Chapel, it didn't work the way they had expected or hoped. Yes, they did skip the line at the ticket booth (easily a couple of hours) but they couldn't avoid the line *inside* the museum and in the un-air conditioned 'Sardine Chapel' as it's been referred to in other places. It was the one blot on their otherwise perfect vacation.

I've got to say, Europe (particularly Italy) is extremely popular with tourists and travellers. It's not an exaggeration to say that they come by the bus loads and boat loads. This means that many of the places and attractions that bring people to Europe can get crowded to and beyond the max. If you're not prepared, it can make for a lot of frustration and wasted time. In a perfect world we should be able to walk right through the doors of the Musée d'Orsay in Paris (or other equally popular spots) and then have the place to ourselves to enjoy. Sorry it doesn't work that way. However, there are ways to make it a little less irritating.

One way to do this is to travel in the off-season. When the weather is cold and dreary the crowds disappear for some reason. If you don't care for or dislike hot weather, travel between mid-October and mid-April and you could end up having a popular place pretty much all to yourself. However, if you like hot/ warm weather as part of your holiday, this probably won't work for you.

Another approach is to visit the popular sites either early in the morning or later in the afternoon. A place like St Peter's in Rome can be quite empty of visitors at 7:30 a.m. If you can get going early you can be there while others are still working on their continental breakfasts. Admittedly this isn't for everybody or everywhere but it is one way to beat the crowds. While others are lined up to see a popular site or museum you can be sitting in a piazza enjoying a cool drink while practicing your people watching skills. A little tip: try Piazza Navona in Rome.

If you can get yourself organized before you leave home, make an advance reservation for some of the more crowded locales you would like to see. For example, the Uffizi Gallery in Florence is one of the busiest attractions in the world and can experience lineups of well over three hours in the high season. If you buy a reservation before you leave home, you can stroll right by the vast multitudes and walk right in the door. You'll be walking out about the same time the people you passed in the lineup are getting to the entry door. This, of course means that you'll have first choice for the best people watching spots at the local sidewalk cafés. It does cost more, but why waste time in a lineup when your holiday is already too short. Also, some places only allow people with reservations to enter. Places like the Borghese Gallery in Rome and Leonardo's 'Last Supper' in Milano.

One other way to beat the crowds is to buy a city's multi-attraction pass (tourist cards) that allow you to enter any site, attraction, or museum that participates in the pass. The best one here that I can think of is the Paris Pass. I used one a few Augusts ago when we went to visit the aforementioned Musée D'Orsay. The day we went the lineup was being measured in hours. We walked right by the lineup, went through the door, through security and we were in! We had arranged the Pass before we left home and had it delivered to our hotel room. It was waiting for us when we arrived from Antibes. Again, you pay for this, and it doesn't offer relief from crowds once you enter the attraction, but at least you haven't already wasted two hours in a line to buy a ticket.

Summer sun and crowds just seem to go together. In some cases (the Vatican and Versailles come to mind) the institutions you're visiting are not very good at managing crowds within their limited capacity. I know the last time I was at Versailles, I was so concerned with the crowding that I thought the place dangerous. Even Paris' Rodin Museum was crowded, but luckily most of the things we wanted to see were in the park that forms part of the Museum estate. Anything you can do to avoid the crowds is to your advantage. Be smart, where there's a lineup there's usually a way to avoid it.

22.
TRAVEL COSTS

NOBODY LIKES ugly surprises. Some people return from a trip they've really enjoyed and find that they blew way past their budget guestimates. That can be a real downer. On the other hand, some of us may practice 'magical budgeting'. That's the purposeful under-estimating of our probable costs so we can justify the travel. If that's your practice then invariably, 'ugly' follows 'magical'. If that's what you do, it's ugly but not a surprise.

When you make an honest mistake and find out you spent too much, we hope you can do better the next time. To do that you need to get better at determining what your cost elements are and how much you'll spend on each.

First, here's a list of just some of the common things people spend money on when they travel and should be allowed for in a budget:

- Flights, both long haul and local, including all fees for baggage, drinks, etc.
- Checked luggage costs
- Airport car parking
- Accommodations (best use a daily average cost times the number of days)
- Local transportation such as car rentals, ferries, trains, taxis and hired transfers
- Meals, snacks and street food, and drinks (estimate a cost per day times the number of days)
- Souvenirs, trinkets and trash

- Entrance fees, passes, entertainment, guides and local tours

- Travel Insurance

- Phones and communications (cell service and internet access is never free)

- Gratuities and tips

- Maintenance and laundry

- Currency exchange costs

- Contingency reserves

- Agency fees

- Big things like cruise costs if applicable

When you do travel, keep all your receipts, don't guess.

A well-designed Excel work sheet can be a great help. Allow not only a budget number for each cost element but also a place to record expenses so that you can compare the results. After you return home, spend a few minutes to put the costs against the plan and see what you guessed right and what you guessed wrong. It will give you a better idea of what you might do the next time. The better you get at this the more travel you may be able to enjoy. Bon Voyage!

23.
LEAVING A FOOTPRINT

OVER THE last few years, the question of climate change has come to the fore as it concerns travel, thanks to Greta Thunberg and others!

There is little doubt that travel generates greenhouse gases that contribute to global warming. On the other hand, there is no doubt travel can make a positive contribution to peace and our understanding of the world we live in and the other people with whom we share this planet. These are competing demands and we must find a way to satisfy both.

While technology may help eventually, we need to improve the way we use resources today by modifying some of the things we currently do. While we shouldn't need to stop travelling, we do need to do it better and with more consideration. One area that could be curtailed significantly is business travel. I have some experience in this matter, as I was at one time a senior executive for a Canadian owned freight business with partners around the world. I admit I enjoyed some of the travel but I also think that there are now better alternatives to face to face meeting.. Improvements to telecommunications in the last thirty years have been mind boggling.

Personal travel for leisure purposes could be done better with a little forethought. Better planning up front, more focus on how we can move around efficiently and a more thoughtful use of resources at our destinations will all make a positive contribution to reducing pollution. Travel Advisors need to be trained to help people do this.

The following chart is a recent list of the percentages of total greenhouse gas (GHGs) emissions generated by types of transportation:

Cars	40%
Trucks	34%
Planes	11%
Boats	11%
Trains	4 %

Now here's a list from the European Community's Department of Business Energy and Industrial Strategy of "Emissions **per passenger per km travelled**" for different modes of transportation:

Short haul flights	133g of CO_2
Long haul flights	102g of CO_2
Car with 1 pax	171g of CO_2
Car with 4 pax	43g of CO_2
City bus	104g of CO_2
Intercity bus	27g of CO_2
Eurostar HS rail	6g of CO_2

If you were going from Paris to Nice on the TGV, it takes about five hours and 30 minutes to cover a distance of 687 km, generating about 4,122g of CO_2 per passenger.

The same route by plane (short haul) is the same distance and flying time is one hour 25 minutes and you'll generate 91,371g of CO_2 per passenger. This time doesn't include to/from airports. If you add in the time to get to the airport, check in and load, and reverse at the other end you take close to the same time as the trains, which go downtown to downtown.

The same trip for four passengers in a car takes about nine hours to cover 931 km and generates a total of 30,033g of CO_2.

You choose which is best for the environment, or which is the quickest. Any way you look at it, use the train if you can for this type of trip. You can use the same planning considerations for any trip you want to take. You should note that the train is powered by electricity, most of which is generated by non-carbon-based fuels, i.e., electricity. Yes, it helps to know how the electricity is generated. Slower diesel-powered trains have a higher CO_2 output.

As a general rule of thumb, you don't lose much by being climate conscious when you move about. There's still a lot more information needed by the public before they can become environmentally efficient, but it's coming.

Things are still early in the attempt to make travel friendlier to the environment As you think about the trade-offs, try to make the climate healthier.

24.
DRIVERS – START YOUR ENGINES!

DRIVING IN Europe can be fun…or really terrifying! Probably both. It depends how you approach it. The French do it with savoir faire, the Germans do it as fast as they can, Italians are just plain crazy and the English don't even know they're on the wrong side of the road! North Americans usually find it a bit of a challenge.

The first time I drove in Europe, in 1976, I picked up a rental car at Gatwick airport, and my wife at the time, new to navigating, took me on the shortest route she saw on her map, north to Dunstable. A quick look at Google's maps will show you that we went right through the middle of downtown London. I was just getting used to the right-hand drive with a gear shift to the left of the steering wheel when we got to the centre of the city. Talk about a baptism of fire! We survived that experience, the marriage didn't, but I've since had many enjoyable road trips in the UK and Western Europe and feel quite comfortable driving anywhere over there.

Within reason, most North Americans can make their way safely through any Western European country side, but it is advisable not to drive in the core parts of major cities such as Paris, Rome, Berlin, and Milan. I used to tell my clients, "fly into any big city, spend your time there, then go back to the airport, pick up your rental car and head to the boondocks and keep your sanity."

You need to do some research before picking up a rental and heading off to the European hinterland. The driving rules are different than those here. They use a lot more cameras to control speeding (it doesn't work on Italians) and yet their speed limits are much higher than here. In Italy, tailgating is a common and an honourable preparation for the Formula 1 circuit that they all aspire to be a part of soon. No right turns on red lights over there. Many city centres in

Italy are closed to non-resident drivers. If you see a sign that says "ZTL" don't go any further!

Navigating can be fun over there. Many towns, villages and cities have been in the same place for centuries. However, it's common practice to not have some of the roads appear on the GPS at all. I suspect that some local authorities don't tell anybody when they make a change to their road network, so the GPS makers can be left in the dark. You also need to realize that your GPS can't pick up a satellite signal in a tunnel hundreds of feet inside a mountain. Just for fun, I think, the road builders created a split in the tunnel, one way to go north and one way to go east with some signage that uses a series of names for remote villages you've never heard of. Between Germany, Switzerland, Austria, and Italy there are many mountains; so be warned, take a map with you.

If you want a real challenge, take a seven-passenger van from Sorrento and take it along the Amalfi Coast to at least Positano. If you survive that you are a true professional driver.

As a final word, some people can be stupid at times. Don't let it be you. Don't drink any alcohol and drive, period. Most of Europe uses .05 as the upper level of alcohol in your blood for impaired driving.

25.
TRAINS AND BOATS AND ... BUSES?

I KNOW, I know...the original song was written in 1965 by Burt Bacharach and Hal David for Gene Pitney, who never did record it! I changed the title slightly for my purposes.

As a traveller, I've used most of the various modes of transportation to get around my geographical area of expertise. I've taken long distance trains, high speed trains and local commuter trains. I've taken a ferry across the English Channel and little rivers (but never the Mersey). I've flown extensively but I've never experienced a European intercity bus!

As a Travel Advisor, buses were not something we could easily arrange and it was not something most of my clients asked for. Additionally, up until the early 2010s, and later in some places, intercity coach services were government regulated in much of Europe by national governments, most of whom were more intent on developing fast intercity rail networks instead. In the few years since they were deregulated, coach networks have blossomed and are now a viable way of getting around short and medium distances. There are even some overnight sleeper buses. Costs are relatively low, but especially for a traveller with limited time, trains, particularly high speed trains are still the best way to move between major centres. A number of bus companies have sprung up based in the major nations and are developing extensive domestic and some international routes. Here are some of the more prominent names:

- France – Ouibus, a subsidiary of SNCF the French national rail operator.

- Flixbus – a German operator.

- Regio Jet – a Czech operator.

- Eurolines – European wide operator.

- National Express – a long-time UK bus company.

Today, all of these companies are online and tickets can be purchased from them at their websites. These operators are Europe's version of Greyhound. Few Travel Advisors are knowledgeable about these so you're best to make your own arrangements for these operations. I should note, these operators are not the same as the companies that use coaches for organized escorted group tours with guides and a pre-booked packaged itinerary.

There's not much to say about ferry operations. Generally, they are specific to certain routes, countries and regions. Some can be booked in advance and some are walk-on operators. Greece is one of the countries with extensive operations but there are many others, usually in countries with extensive island networks such as the Philippines and Indonesia. In all cases, you should make yourself familiar with their safety records, as the less developed the country, the slacker the enforcement of their safety regulations.

I really enjoy modern long-distance trains. No stress, good on-time performance (when not on strike - France!), and safe and comfortable at reasonable prices. The crème de la crème are the high speed operations such as Eurostar and TGV. Even the Germans have developed a highly efficient high-speed rail network. One rail feature most people are aware of are some of the higher end tourist rail operations, such as Rocky Mountaineer, the Orient Express, Australia's Ghan (Adelaide to Cairns) and the Sydney to Perth run on the Indian Pacific. All these are available through a knowledgeable Travel Advisor.

All of these operators take the stress out of driving and navigating in strange places. It's off your shoulders. Your personal travel should be relaxing.

26.
BEWARE THE MARKETING!

THERE ARE certain realities I've learned about travel marketing practices over the last thirty years.

In travel, the best value, high quality travel experiences never go on sale. They sell out before there's any need for discounting. Conversely, the least attractive, scuzzy, all-inclusive resort will always be on sale. Comparatively low pricing is always a sign of comparatively low quality. "You get what you pay for."

In fact, if you run into an unbelievably good price on a high-quality product, it's probably a mistake. Some years ago, my agency in Victoria partnered with a nationally prominent sun destination tour operator for an advertising campaign. The tour operator controls the price as they are the party at risk. This tour operator made a mistake and advertised in our local paper a good quality all-inclusive resort for a two-week duration at the one-week price! Now you should know that at that time, a newspaper ad might generate a few phone calls and maybe two or three sales. This tour operator honoured the price and we made almost twenty sales in less than a week! Customers know a good thing when they see it.

I am of the opinion that for a traveller to get what they want, when they want it, they need to be prepared to pay a fair price, not a stupidly high price or a stupidly low price but a fair price. Everybody understands that an air fare to London, England from Toronto is lower in the winter than it is in the summer. Demand makes it easier to sell seats during school holidays. Conversely cruise prices into the Caribbean around school spring breaks tend to be firm as demand is high. There may be last minute sales but they'll be for things like inside cabins on older ships.

Where travellers need to be prepared to dig a little deeper in their research is when certain products tend to be over-hyped or plain old misrepresented. This happens with some hotels. Their websites show pictures of nice rooms on sunny days after a real good cleaning and maybe even a fresh paint job. They may forget to tell you they haven't refreshed the rooms in four years and things are a little worn and they haven't updated their photos. Some properties are not beyond using influencers to hype a place you wouldn't send your worst enemy to. While some travel sites show a whole bunch of good comments rating a property, read them with a grain of salt! It's happened that some hotels pay for some of these ratings, or discount the next room for a positive comment.

One set of researchers found that hotel marketing practices increasingly depend on peers' opinions and online ratings. The results also suggest that rating lists are more believable when published by well-known authentic authoritative travel sites and publications. Favourable attitudes toward a hotel and higher booking intentions are revealed when the hotel appears in best hotels lists such as Conde Nast magazines' ratings. Yet, some hoteliers do lie! Some hoteliers do ask their friends and employees for rave reviews. Besides online lists, check out other rating systems and sites for their views. Guide books like Rick Steves' series are good; just don't expect all the ratings to be current for more than a year. Michelin is still the best source for restaurant ratings.

Be careful out there! Beware the unscrupulous operators and the inexperienced travellers, they know not what they're talking about.

And remember, all advertising is self-serving to some extent!

27.
BUYER BEWARE!

THIS IS about a story from the Toronto Star printed a few years ago.

A couple booked an all-inclusive Christmas vacation with Air Canada Vacations in Cuba and paid over $3,000 for the package. You need to know that Air Canada Vacations is a separate 'legal' entity wholly owned by the airline and operating as a tour operator. A tour operator (also sometimes known as a whole-saler) is a packager of travel components, such as flights, hotels, transfers, and attractions. Usually they sell the package for one all-inclusive price, although some can also sell individual components if they have the agreement of the primary provider/operator.

When these people arrived at their destination, they found that the resort hotel was full and they couldn't get the first class room they had reserved. When offered inferior accommodations in lieu, they refused the offer and flew home the same day they had arrived.

Once home they sued the tour operator Air Canada Vacations in small claims court and won $4,200 as a refund and to cover their out of pocket expenses for the new flight home.

But, and it's a big but, Air Canada Vacations appealed the small claims court decision and won. The traveller ended up having to pay Air Canada Vacations' legal costs of over $9,500! They didn't get what they originally paid for and they ended up down over $12,500 for a holiday they didn't get. What happened here? This doesn't sound right now does it?

Without going into the gory details, the appeals court ruled that Air Canada Vacations had no duty of care to clients. In essence, the court said that Air

Canada Vacations did not have to supervise a third-party supplier (the hotel) and that the tour operators must only make reasonable efforts to find a competent contractor and once that is done their responsibility ends there. The court held that it was established common law that it was impractical to impose the onerous duty on the tour operator to supervise the day to day activities of an independent contractor. Also, the tour operator's terms and conditions stated this, allowing the company to deny responsibility for costs arising out of this type of poor performance (and a whole bunch of other nasty stuff!). If you need to know more, talk to a lawyer with an expertise in travel contracts and if it gets to that level, it's well past a Travel Advisor's pay grade!

Since these types of winter sun holidays are particularly popular with Canadians, here are some thoughts on how to shift the odds a little more in your favour:

- First: Read and understand the terms and conditions of the holiday package you're buying. Each tour operator has this information on their website and in the back of their brochures. Look at them carefully and make sure you can live with them. Remember that the tour operator's lawyer wrote these to protect the tour operator, not you.

- Second: Use a tour operator who still uses Destination Representatives. These are employees of the tour operator who are located in the destination for the express purpose of helping travellers who may have problems. Better to catch a problem early and certainly you don't want to let it fester until you get home.

- Third: If you do have a problem at the destination make sure you get all the details of the parties involved including legal names of hotels, etc., addresses and contact information, as you'll need them when you get home. Make it a priority when you get home to complain in writing to the tour operator.

- Fourth: If you live in Ontario, Quebec, or British Columbia there are provincial regulators who may be able to help sort out problems you encounter with travel agents or tour operators. If dealing directly with the tour operator doesn't solve the problem, then turn to these government bodies for assistance and help.

- Fifth: Don't throw away the invoice your travel agent gave you for the trip. It is proof of a contract and should contain the details of what you booked. You'll need it in Ontario and other regulated provinces to prove you had a contract and are covered to whatever extent the contract calls for.

- Finally: Spend a little money and consult a lawyer before you start a claim in small claims court. If nothing else they may save you from making an expensive mistake such as this couple did. In fact, the lawyer might be able to help you make a claim against a hotel directly in a Canadian court if it comes to that. Collecting on a win may be another thing all together.

The three big provinces, Ontario, Quebec, and BC all have regulatory bodies that certify and discipline travel agents and tour operators doing business in their province. In each province they also operate a fund to protect consumers from failures and non-performance of travel agencies in their province. In BC, the body is called Consumer Protection BC and is government operated. In Ontario, it is called TICO, meaning Travel Industry Council of Ontario and is a self-regulating body whose members are partly elected by travel businesses and others appointed by the government. In Quebec, it is the Office of Consumer Protection (OPC). All are designed to protect consumers, collect funds from travel agents to run their operations, to licence and qualify individuals and businesses and reimburse travellers in cases where the travel operator fails to meet their obligations. Anywhere else in Canada it's 'anything goes'!

SECTION B
TRAVEL ADVISORS

1.

WHERE ARE YOU GOING?

IF YOU don't know where you're going, you'll never get there. If you want a successful career as a Travel Advisor, somewhere along the line you'll need to make some decisions about what you want to be good at!

If you believe you can know the whole world and all the travel possibilities it represents, you'll need to give it a bit of a rethink. In travel, being a jack of all trades means you're a master of none. This was the old approach to being a 'travel agent' where you really worked on behalf of the travel suppliers and your need for a detailed understanding of specific travel subjects wasn't as important as being able to book a bunch of different suppliers and get paid by the supplier. While that is still a fair part of the trade, particularly for new entrants, that role is getting smaller and smaller as suppliers reduce what they are willing to pay for your services and where the client can almost always easily deal directly with any supplier anywhere in the world. You need to be a resource to the client, where they pay you directly and you're responsible for the advice you give.

To be a long-term success in the Travel Advisor role, you now need to be able to create unique travel experiences in at least a couple of specific areas such as a destination specialist, or an air fare expert, or as a specialist in corporate travel and so forth. Yes, you'll also handle the mundane simple air fares from Toronto to Vancouver, but don't expect to make enough money at it to survive.

If you're a new entrant to the industry, take a couple of years as a travel agent to get a clear understanding of the work, then you should start focusing your efforts on a couple of specific aspects of the business. You need a plan. Here are a couple of questions that will help you on your way:

- What do you want to be when you grow up? What are you really good at? More important, what interests you? Narrow it down to no more than two or three specialties.

- What are the key specific steps you need to take?

- How are you going to get there?

- How will you know when you have arrived?

- Are you willing to invest your own resources to travel that specialty yourself?

- It's your life. What is it about travel you love? Are you interested enough to concentrate on that manner of travel?

On a personal note, I was in my early forties when I entered the business. I had worked as an executive in the logistics business and had travelled extensively in North America and Europe over a period of nearly twenty years and loved the experiences. It took me a few years but as I most enjoyed France and especially Italy, I decided they would be the specialties I would personally focus on. It made sense even though there was a lot of competition. The market to those parts of Europe is enormous and I had a lot of personal experience travelling to those places. I could build around that!

I did have a couple of other destinations in my back pocket but they weren't popular with Canadian travellers at that time. I avoided most of Asia, Africa, and South America as I had never been there and they weren't destinations that caught my personal attention. Other people who worked with me had and I left most of that business to them. Simple air fares to those destinations were okay for me, but others in the agency were the experts.

Each person in the industry should have their own strategic plan for their special approach to travel and work it starting from early in their career so that they become known for something special.

2.
HEY, TRAVEL ADVISOR -
HAVE YOU THOUGHT ABOUT THIS?

YOU NEED to understand that a 'do everything for everybody' approach isn't a road to long term success and personal satisfaction in today's travel business. If you're currently in the business, have you ever said no, you don't do something or don't have the expertise to help a customer with a requested travel booking?

You need an approach that makes you stand out to your customers, gives them a reason to work with you and makes you different than other travel agents and Advisors. You need a competitive strategy. That book, "Competitive Strategy" (all 400 pages), was written back in 1980 by a guy named Michael Porter at Harvard. Although focused at a different level of business, he produced and codified some pretty basic ideas about competitive strategies. His premise was that there are three basic competitive, strategic approaches and you need to choose one.

The first one he enumerated was overall 'Cost' leadership. Note, he didn't say lowest price, as he was focused on the long-term benefits of better profitability. It's hard to imagine this approach working well in the local travel agency/ Advisor business as the supplier world is loath to substantially prefer one agency or Advisor over another unless you have built a book of business that is literally second to none in size. However, Expedia and others used this route on their way to being online behemoths. They strive to keep costs down through converting people to self-service. They have good prices, but lower costs per transaction and so are able to be highly price competitive. In terms of costs to operate a local agency/Advisor business, there is little room to maneuver your costs for things like rent, phones and so forth, in order to be substantially below those of a competitor and so that you can build your pricing approach.

The second approach Porter mentions is 'Differentiation'. What do you do for the customer that others don't or can't? In the travel business this means can you focus your business on specific destinations, specific forms of travel such as cruising or weddings or complicated air itineraries? Can you make a viable business by holding yourself out as a specialist in travel to Italy? Is that market big enough? Can you build a substantial position in the cruise business or with a specific cruise line in your market? Destination weddings are hot right now. Will that business be enough?

The third generic competitive strategy is 'Focus' which really is a combination of where you develop your business for a specific group of customers involved in a specific activity. For example, some agencies have developed cost effective strong businesses on specific ethnic air markets. Others have focused on the LGBT community cruisers, others look for growth specializing on conferences, while others build their business by combining business meetings with a cruising conference.

Many agents and agencies start out with building a business in a local neighbourhood market but eventually are hurt by other operators who have a more specific strategy. These local businesses tend to last only as long as the owner wants to stay in business and people value their proximity. Developments over the last twenty years show that this isn't a formula for long term growth and success. Things happen that can cause the business to fail as it either gets smaller, agents retire or work from home, or it gets taken out at a low price by a larger operator. Individual Advisors should also give some thought to these questions.

The more clearly a market understands what you do well, the better your chances of long-term success.

3.
HAVE YOU THOUGHT OF THIS –
PART 2?

WHEN YOU want to grow and develop your business, the first question you as a Travel Advisor, should ask yourself, after you've gone from being an agent to an Advisor, is, "why me"? Why should a potential client choose you to handle their travel?

A new travel agent needs to gain experience in a wide range of travel clients, products, and destinations before they can make a decision about the prime thing they may want to specialize in. Some people, particularly those mature individuals who enter the business in mid-life may already have a good idea of what they want to do, but a newbie should get a couple of years under their belts before they focus on one aspect of the business. Even if you do become a specialist, you'll have many opportunities to handle travel that is not part of your prime focus.

Why should a potential new client choose to do business with you? Why should they come to you, specifically, when they need help to plan their travel? What makes you different from the other people in the business? Do you want to focus on one type of client or on one form of travel experience or one destination?

Some Advisors will do a lot of different types of travel for a client, regardless of their own interests, knowledge, experience, and training. They work at 'collecting' clients and arranging any travel the client wants to do. If that's the case, the Advisor should 'focus' on the type of clients they collect and if possible, on the type of travel they want. Otherwise, you may be mediocre at what you do for a living. This is not a formula for long term success.

Other Travel Advisors want to help with one specific form of travel, such as:

- Cruising

- Sun/Resort holidays

- Groups

- Honeymoons and Weddings

- Luxury

- Disney

- River cruising

- Business travel

- Adventure.

This list is not all inclusive. While these can be high volume forms of travel, you'll need a client population base large enough to justify the focus.

Some travellers like to work with an Advisor who has specialist knowledge of a specific region or destination. Needless to say, if this is your approach, you'll need to have visited the destination a 'few' times. Nobody is going to believe you unless you can say you've seen the place and have some first-hand knowledge. Once you've done that and studied the destination and visited it a number of times, you'll need to keep current through research and travel. Having a second language helps too, although it is not an impediment if you don't. Remember that you need to be able to communicate to your clients some authority about the destination. A good command of the English language is more important than having some language skills for the destination. In my own case, I focused on Italy and Western Europe. Before entering the travel business, I had travelled Europe extensively for business and made the destination decision as it was a place I knew and enjoyed. My own experience convinced me that if you are going to be a destination specialist you need to visit the destination <u>at least</u> every two to three years.

Whatever you decide, be consistent with the messages you send to promote your choice. Nobody can be all things to all people. Make a choice, work it as hard as you can, and give it time to grow.

4.

INTANGIBLE SERVICE AND TRUST

MY WIFE and I went into a mall in the small city of Welland the other day to ask people at our cell phone provider, Fido, to help us set up some new phones we'd ordered online. We've been Fido clients for more than ten years. Neither of us are technically oriented, me even less than she is. We were supposed to do it ourselves as part of the deal, but we didn't seem to have the necessary 'secret decoder ring' or the knowledge to make it happen. The guy who helped us was Trevor, the supervisor of the outlet and he was a good guy. Fido is a cell phone service provider, and I have to say Trevor understood the concept of service. It took a while but by the time Trevor was finished we went home with perfectly working phones with all the stuff that was in the old ones now in the new ones, no set up fee. Turns out that the 'service part' was as important to Trevor as the 'cell phone' part of the business. Trevor understood this completely and earned our trust.

If you're a Travel Advisor you're in the service business, you just happen to deal in travel. You plan, organize and book travel for people. You sell travel, and you depend on suppliers and others to deliver on your promises. For people to want you to do this for them, they need to trust you! You in turn need to earn the travellers' trust. How do you do this? There are a few things you need to do to earn and keep a client's trust:

- Talk about the traveller, not yourself.

- Ask questions then shut up and listen carefully.

- Don't oversell! Under promise and over perform.

- Explain problems and tell people how you'll solve them.

- Do what you say you'll do.

- Build a history of high-quality experiences for them.

You need to prove your worth. Trust doesn't just appear; it's grown over time. The trustor takes a risk, and the trustee earns it. This takes time to build and a split second to lose.

Building a relationship of trust is the same as building a romance! There are certain things you need to do:

- Take the initiative, nobody wants to date a wimp.

- Illustrate and explain, don't tell, go softly.

- Listen for what's different, don't get surprised.

- Compliments are okay, flattery is not.

- Earn the right to advise. When it's the right time, offer an opinion and justify it.

- Say what you mean, don't be mealy mouthed.

- Be sure your advice is wanted.

- Show appreciation and interest in the people not just their money.

If you're smart about following an approach like this, you'll develop a friendship and a customer and you should have both for a long time.

5.
THE TRAVEL ADVISOR TODAY – WHERE ARE YOU?

IN THE good old days, back before cell phones, Wi-Fi and 'the inter-web', you'd find a traditional leisure-oriented travel agent in a store front office on a main street, with lots of foot traffic going by the door. The least busy agent, not on the phone, handled the next person to walk in, unless the client wanted to wait for their preferred agent.

Things have and are changing, although a lot of agencies still have a store front office. There are many more ways and places for a client to find highly capable Travel Advisors. Instead of just in a local phone book, Travel Advisors in your local area or anywhere else in the world should be found where people want to look. The internet is full of them, but which one is the right one? Are you the right one for the particular client's needs? Do you really want the business if they need someone who's knowledgeable of South America and you specialize in Japan? Today agents can be found in storefronts, call centres or in any one of a multitude of online listings by aggregators. However, is that the best way for a client to find a true Travel Advisor?

If you're an Advisor associated with a retail agency, clients can usually find you through the agency. If you're a home based/outside Advisor, they may need to look a little deeper. I do believe that the most rewarding business results for both travellers and Advisors comes from long-standing, trust-infused working friendships between clients and Advisors. Would you want to work with a lawyer, accountant, or doctor 3000 miles away? The opportunities for misunderstandings are many, just like a long-distance romance! It doesn't matter how good your electronics are.

The absolute best way to build a strong, lasting commercial relationship with a client is to meet them face to face, on an as needed basis. The way to secure a client's support is to meet, establishing excellent verbal interpersonal communications. It allows for active listening, reading of body language and non-verbal expressions, and to be empathetic to what a person is saying.

As an Advisor I always wanted to meet the client on his or her ground. For one thing, in Ontario it can get you in trouble with TICO, the provincial regulator, if you meet at your place of residence. You need to be very careful; do house calls. By meeting your client on their home ground, you get a more comprehensive feel for who they are and what is important to them. For some clients, seeing an agent's disorganized sloppy office does not engender confidence. Personal, big money spends by clients are not something they want you to take a casual approach to.

Personally, I found the client's residence/work locations or a Starbucks/ Timmy's to be the best places to make the client feel comfortable and for you to introduce your skills and knowledge regarding their plans. If you need to work further you can move much of your detailed communications over to your email or a phone. When you're finished your bookings, always present your document package (even the electronic versions) to the client in person. We'll talk about that in a lot more detail in another segment.

Remember, if a client wanted an electronic agent they could have looked to Expedia!

6.
WORDS, TICS AND TELLS!

IN OVER 25 years as a Travel Advisor, I can't remember a single incident where a leisure client came to me with a detailed written description of the trip they wanted to take. It may have happened, I am getting old, yet, I can't remember it happening, even once! With a vast number of my clients, the discussion tended to follow the same simple pattern where the client told me what they wanted to do, in as much detail as they had thought it through. Often it was not much. I then asked a lot of questions and got a good understanding of what was needed and who the person or people were as travellers and as individuals. Quite often, the meeting led to interesting conversations about other things the client was interested in doing.

In most cases, we started with a face to face discussion and followed up with a number of phone calls or more face to face conversations. Sometimes they made an appointment by phone, but in the majority of cases it was a drop in. Subsequent trips may have started with a phone call, but I have to say I always would prefer a personal meeting, and usually managed to get at least one before making reservations for a trip. In fact, a lot of the meetings were over a coffee at the client's residence, or Timmy's, or Starbucks.

When you meet face to face with a client and discuss their plans, needs, and travel dreams you get a much richer understanding of where they're coming from, and going to. Words are words, but they're much richer in meaning when you can see the expressions, body language, tics and tells that give you a deeper understanding of who the person or people are and what they really want. Their reactions, feelings, enthusiasms, fears, and desires often only surface when you can see the person. Gestures, facial expressions, and posture all enrich the communications and add to a listener's comprehension. Are their arms crossed, are they tapping their fingers, tenting their fingers, head tilting to the side, rubbing their hands together, or cradling their chin in their hands? Was I doing any of these things?

If the only time we talked was over the phone I could have missed some of these signs and the understanding I got from the talk was not always accurate or complete. If I missed the full gamut of communications, I also lost the business some of the time. Even if I didn't lose the business, I didn't do it as well as I could have and it cost me a lot of time clarifying and correcting misconceptions.

Phone calls are good where all you need to do is collect details and pass along some information. They are not adequate for discussing information, options, opinions, and recommendations where the client wants to delve more deeply into the subject.

In the last decade or so, as the internet gained acceptance as a marketplace, the dominant trend has been for people to book either simple, single travel items such as flights or hotels and sometimes packages like sun resorts. Yet it isn't a good tool for travellers who want a complicated set of arrangements for an important trip or where risks to smooth travel may be involved. Someone coined the term 'hate selling' to describe all the anti-consumer techniques used by many booking sites to push shoppers to a purchase. A conversation with a website about the details of travel is a sure lead into disaster. FAQs are not a conversation and do not lead to clarity. Your advantage as a Travel Advisor is that you can deal with subtlety, complexity, and confusion that no site can match. Play to that strength.

7.
DESIGNING TRAVEL AND
YOUR REPUTATION

AS A Travel Advisor I had many interesting conversations with clients trying to determine what they wanted out of a trip and if the resources were available to do what they wanted. Most people were reasonable and were understanding of the constraints involved. Still, most assignments involved negotiating trade-offs, the majority of which dealt with time. Money wasn't always the biggest constraint to travel for people; available time was almost always a problem.

Being a Travel Advisor means you spend a great deal of your time designing the travel experiences of others around their interests and specifications. For most of these tasks you need to work around at least two or three key parameters: interests, time, and money. Two of these criteria are limiting and provide outside boundaries: the time available and the budget. Yet, their interests can be multiple and unlimited. So much so, that many times I found myself advising a client to, "Save that for the next time, you'll want to go back."

Your task is best approached by using a process that will provide the travel experiences within time and money available. Here is a suggestion of an approach you can take.

After your conversation with the client, start your research on the experiences the client wishes. Make note of the time needed and the costs to be incurred. If for example a client wants to visit the Ferrari facilities in Maranello while they're in Tuscany, how much time is needed there and in transit to/from the facility and what is the cost? These decisions will help you to define where they'll be, in what sequence and how long they'll need. Too many times I've seen people come in saying, "We'd like three days in Paris and two days in…" without thinking what they'll do in those days. Inevitably, we'd end up re-doing this two or three times before an acceptable solution was found. Sometimes, many times, you'll be asked for your suggestions of where they should spend their activity time. Be ready for the question!

Funnily enough, some people say they don't want to be constrained or over-programmed and will work that out as they go. This can potentially be a bad idea, so don't program them but give them a list of things to do and see and they'll have the opportunity to do them when they're in the mood. Do warn them that some of the more popular things are hampered by long lineups and/or the need for advanced reservations. Find a way to help them understand that the reason for visiting isn't to stay in a hotel but rather to see some of the world they don't normally experience. Their energy levels will determine what they do.

Once you have the activity (and non-activity) time allocated and sequenced and the budget for activities determined, you'll need to discuss it with the client. This is the essence of what the travel is about. Once this is settled you can start working out the logistics of transportation and accommodations and any special specific experiences. While these logistics are the commission generating part of travel for you, the one thing that will enhance your reputation is if you get the experiences right! It's funny but most people can easily forget the name of a hotel they stayed at in Paris after a while, but they'll always remember their visit to the Louvre. For long term success and client satisfaction, tell them what to do!

8.
IF THEY HAVE IT. USE IT!

DEAR TRAVEL ADVISOR:

If you are designing a trip for a client and you don't include something substantial for all five of their senses, you're not doing a complete job! I'm always struck when I hear people talk about their travels when they talk about 'what they saw'. Sometimes, they mention a good meal, less often they mention what they heard and even less frequently what they touched or smelled.

For example, if you're building a trip to Italy (a destination I'm most familiar with), there's a lot to see, and that's an understatement! Art, architecture, people and landscapes are just some of the generics that fill that bill. The Sistine Chapel and St. Peter's in Rome, the Uffizi Gallery in Firenze and St. Marks in Venice are just three of the more well known in the art and architecture category. The Cinque Terre and Tuscany are just a couple of the more striking landscapes of the country.

If you're a fan, Italian food has an enormous range of tastes in food and wine. Not only is the food regional, but so are the beverages. It's pretty easy to add five kg to your body mass on a ten day sojourn to Italia! There's a lot more to it than pizza! Wild boar from Tuscany, 'busiate al pesto Trapanese' from Liguria and the list goes on.

Do the names Vivaldi, Verdi, Puccini, Scarlatti, Rossini, Donizetti, Monteverdi or Morricone mean anything to your ears? Those are just some of the well know dead guys of opera and movie music! Still today there are a lot of young Italians making a life in music today. You may want to know who they are. Can you imagine how much you might enjoy wandering around the back roads of Tuscany in a tiny Fiat Cinquecento listening to Pavarotti singing Puccini's

Nessun Dorma? You've got to try it. I guarantee you'll be breaking the speed limit by the time it's finished.

If you happen to end up in the Oltrarno across the river from Florence and you are passing by a leather shop, stop and go in and just caress one of the leather satchel purses on display. Let your hand carefully trace a line along a stone wall in Pompeii and know that it's been there for more than two thousand years. Do I need to mention silk in a fashion designer's atelier in Milan!

You can't stroll down a street in an Italian town in the morning without smelling an amazing aroma of strong coffee coming from a coffee 'bar' or the scent of vanilla coming from a pasticceria. Walk into an active church and your nose is assaulted by the aromas from the candles.

Your job is to plan the experiences for all senses; plan the trip and give them ideas to check out! Follow-up with the clients on their return. A Travel Advisor should program a trip that takes all the traveller's senses into account. It makes for a much richer experience to be enjoyed by your client.

Sincerely,

John

9.
HAVE I EVER BEEN TO IRELAND?

THE CLIENT asked me if I'd ever been to Ireland. He was thinking of going there and wanted to know what I thought and what I knew of the destination. Little did he know! It doesn't get that interesting or evocative too often. Yes, I said, I have…a couple of times.

The first time was in 2000 when my wife and I landed in Dublin, spent a few days wandering around, did a little business and then picked up a rental car and drove down to Killarney for a couple of days. We wandered around the Dingle Peninsula, then off to Blarney then on to Thomastown to visit my bride's ancestors' plots and Kilkenny for the beer. Finally, back to Dublin and on to other destinations. Some of that trip is memorable and some is lost in the fog of time.

The next year we left Vancouver on September 9th and arrived in Dublin with a group of fifty dentists and some of their wives. We had arranged to start a golf holiday for them over the next week or so. A few dental lectures over the next few days made it a business trip for them and all the tax implications that implied. That night we all went on to the Dublin Literary Pub Crawl and next morning headed to a local 'name' golf course before heading over to Killarney that afternoon. Our two buses stopped just outside Limerick at a roadside pub/restaurant for lunch. The horror movie on the bar's TV was about two airplanes crashing into the New York Twin Towers that morning! For that and a number of other reasons, it was a time I'll never forget.

As you can see, I had a story to tell and it helped me explain what I knew of Ireland, for this traveller. In my years I've used stories frequently to caution novice travellers about some of the complications of travel such as visas, passports, and insurance when clients underestimate their risk. They help explain the 'why' factor.

Storytelling is one of the strongest tools in an Advisor's tool box. There are a number of good reasons why this helps explain travel to people. There are a couple of ways of getting information into a brain; the logical route or the emotional route. Emotions are far stronger and last much longer than facts! People remember stories that combine both emotion and facts better than raw facts. Emotions are the much stronger force in storytelling. Think happiness, sadness, fear, disgust, anger, pride, shame, embarrassment, excitement, and surprise and use them properly.

If you are planning to work as a Travel Advisor, you'll want to develop a set of stories that help you appeal to both the logical and emotional sides of a client. Stories also assist a client to see a travel experience in context, and help them understand a situation better than raw travel facts. A quick reminder: the army had a lot of sayings, one of them being "no names, no pack drills". While you can use a client's story, never use their name unless the named party has agreed. Your own stories are the best.

10.
TALKING TO THE CROWDS

IF THERE'S one thing I don't know about travel it's how to advertise to gain new, lifelong customers. While I had a lot of new, long term clients during my time, to the best of my knowledge, not many of them came because of advertising, but I just don't know. I think most were due to walk-ins or referrals or a good reputation, but I don't know for sure. I've tried direct mail, inserts, flyers and the internet, websites, newspapers, radio, and referral schemes, but never gained the number of new clients I wanted for the money spent. Maybe I expected too much? The most successful travel advertising I experienced was the result of a newspaper pricing mistake! (See: "Beware the Marketing" previous).

My first mistake was not to systematically track the reasons why a client chose our agency. How did they find us? So, learn from my folly. My first piece of advice is, find a way to do this for your business or your individual practice. Find out the name of any client who makes a referral resulting in a call to you; then thank them. What sources do your potential clients consult? Who are your potential clients and where do they hang out? These questions are always a good way to start a conversation with a new client. Who do you have in common?

When you look at newspapers, a bit of a dinosaur media in some peoples' minds, it's not a good medium for an emotional appeal. They are good for specific details and pricing discounts or sales, but not a place to appeal to emotions, i.e. the beauty of the Tuscan countryside. The internet is the same in some ways as a newspaper, lots of information, (too much at times) and the ability to do it yourself. Social media may work for some but it was never anything I felt comfortable with. Direct mail is expensive and not held in much regard by the receiver. Not much of it gets read because it is seen as advertising, not information. Rather, it's assigned directly to the circular file on the floor. A regular well-produced personal newsletter will work better. A real estate agent friend of mine takes this approach and is very successful. For most of us, TV is too expensive and in today's multi-channel universe, too diffused. The one area that did better than others was radio and, even then, it was marginal.

For a couple of years, we did a Monday on-air travel segment with the morning host of a local station and it brought in customers but it wasn't cost sustainable at that time for more than a couple of months a year.

As I said earlier, advertising wasn't one of my strong points but what I did learn was from an American guru who is a big fan of radio. His name was Roy H. Williams of Texas who wrote three books that I always found interesting and useful. They were:

- *The Wizard of Ads*, December 1998.

- *Secret Formulas of the Wizard of Ads*, July 1999.

- *Magical Worlds of the Wizard of Ads*, August 2001.

All three were published by Bard Press of Austin, Texas.

The one way to get past all the guards is by using a personally written letter with a hand addressed envelope so the recipient is intrigued enough to open it and at least see who it is from and maybe start to read it as it should look specifically written to them and not another piece of mass mailing marketing crap. Use it to tell stories. Give the recipients a reason to read it!

11.
TRAVEL TALKS

AS A Travel Advisor you can speak to travellers on a one to one basis (I include couples in this category) about individual travel plans and you can also speak to groups of people, both small and large, about travel.

You'll find that when you're one-on-one, the best talks are when the client does most of the talking.

When it's one (you) speaking to more than one or two, then you'll find that you'll do the majority of the speaking.

I've almost always found that sales were strongest when the client did the talking. The percentages of success with one-on-one sales talks were always high You're usually talking specifics. On the other hand, when talking to groups, the percentages were lower but the total sales could be somewhat higher, if you're really good and lucky! That's because the discussion is likely more generic.

When it's one-on-one, the client usually gives you a lot of specific information to work with, if you ask in a proper manner. When you talk to groups you give them a lot of information and collect relatively little back.

Personally, I preferred the one-on-one approach. Usually I was successful in gaining a new client and was able to give them exactly what they were looking for.

In many cases, when dealing with groups of people travelling together, success came if you were talking to a sponsor who represented the groups' interests. We tried a couple of times to generate groups on our own without a sponsor and found little success. When we had a client sponsor, we were quite successful. We took a lot of dentists to Scotland a number of times thanks to the help of a local dental lab. We tried to form our own groups to Mexico but without a sponsor, nothing came from our efforts. It always worked better when we had a 'pied piper'.

Some agencies brought in supplier representatives to do the talking and their own people hung around the periphery to have individual discussions with the audience members after the speaker had concluded. I don't know how successful this was in selling the specific product that was usually the subject of the talk and more importantly how successful it was in developing long term relationships with the travellers.

Group travel can be fun and profitable but it is not easy or simple to create.

12.
WHAT DOES THE CLIENT WANT?

AS A Travel Advisor, no doubt that at one time or another, you'll have a client in front of you and you'll ask yourself, "what do they want me to do?" Two things you need to realize: many times they don't know what they really want and they're not sure what you can and can't do for them. The more experienced travellers they are, the easier it is for them to answer that for themselves. For first timers, a first trip or a new destination can be a concern.

Many a time I've had a person sit down in my office and after the preliminary pleasantries I'd ask, "what would you like me to do for you?" and the answer at times was "I'm not sure. We want to go to Europe, it'll be the first time and we're not far into our plans. We have some questions and concerns."

A professional sales person will commonly refer to these types of client questions as FUDs, meaning 'fears, uncertainties, and doubts'. Before you get into the travel details, deal first with these as much as you can. For example, a few I've heard in my time were:

"Will it be a problem if I can't speak the language?" (Answer: It's usually not that big of a problem).

"What can I do to keep the kids interested while we tour the Loire Valley? There are only so many Chateaux we can see before they get bored." (Answer: Take a hot air balloon ride, if money isn't a big problem).

"My mother is not well and we're a little concerned about being away." (Answer: Check out travel cancellation and trip interruption insurance.)

"My father is terminally ill; can I take him to Alaska?" (Answer: Sorry, there's not much I can do.) (It's a long story, but the cruise line wasn't willing to have him aboard).

Once you are able to set their mind at ease, with no lies, little sugar coating, and as much reassurance as you feel is appropriate, working out the travel program will be much more positive and productive.

If on the other hand they don't know what they want, ask a few questions to start. Where did you go on your last trip? What did you like about it? What didn't you like and what do you do when you're not working. Substitute another word if they're retired. You'll get a lot of hints that might point you in the right direction.

"My fiancé and I are getting married and we want to have the wedding in Tuscany and have our friends and families join us at a villa in Tuscany. Can you help us?" Being a Travel Advisor, but not a priest, I took care of the travel and logistics and pointed her toward a source that helped her with the religious and legal aspects of foreigners getting married in 'Bella Italia'.

Frequently helping people travel means educating them about what you can and can't do and helping them deal with their FUDs.

13.
BECAUSE ... WHICH MEANS...?

FOR A Travel Advisor, sometimes things can seem so simple that we can forget that there are people who don't have the knowledge, experience, or background to comprehend what you're trying to tell them about a trip. It's your job to protect them from nasty surprises.

For example, you're explaining to a client that on a seven-day cruise, the cruise line is offering a prepaid drinks package of only $98 dollars per person (let me know if you can actually find one at that low of a price!). So what? As a savvy Advisor you say to the client, "the package is $98 *which means* you'll get an average of two drinks per day, that usually cost about $7 per drink over seven days." Then the client can understand the value you're talking about and decide if it makes sense to buy it.

Often sales people, including Travel Advisors, assume the client understands what they are being told. That's not always the case, particularly for long or complicated trips. This doesn't apply solely to pricing issues either. Border complications, security concerns, airline connections, and numerous other aspects of travel may confuse travellers and it is your responsibility to test their comprehension and understanding and to provide clear explanations, options, and consequences to your clients. Things like 'non-refundable, no changes allowed' seem to be clear, but many people will still wonder what the exceptions might be. They are not stupid; they just don't have the experience and background to comprehend the problems they might face.

Take travel insurance. Not only is it an Advisor's responsibility to explain what a policy covers, but you must also clearly tell them what is excluded. Never lead them down the garden path of simplicity, for both your own and their sake!

When you're talking about hotels, explain what's included and what extras (like resort fees) might apply to them.

All-inclusive resorts do exclude certain things and it's the Advisor's duty to mention those. There is no room for ambiguity.

Cruises are one of the biggest types of supplier offenders to forget to mention things that may need better explanation. Cruises used to be all inclusive, but have trended over the last few years to exclude many things and make others an extra and high cost. Make sure you let your client know what is extra, as what they don't know may hurt them!

It's an Advisor's responsibility to be thorough and comprehensive in their briefing and explanations for their clients. A client should never be surprised by something you forgot to mention!

14.
BEFORE THEY GO!

ONE OF the most important tasks you do as a Travel Advisor for a client is prepare their 'documentation' for a trip, and then brief the traveller on its contents. This is a serious duty and should never be shoved off by handing the information to the traveller and then saying, "call me if you have questions." I've seen it done! We need to take this responsibility seriously, regardless of how experienced the traveller may be. An Advisor must realize many people can't commit all the details and information about their travel to memory and often need an aide-memoir to help things go smoothly. Whether it's a paper package or a set of e-documentation (most times it should be both), never send a client off without a complete set of information about their travels and a detailed briefing and Q&A session about what's going to happen.

It is best to bind a paper copy set of documents in a soft cover binding that keeps things in order and allows for easy storage in their carry-on. Having the information well organized and sequenced will help take the stress out of their travels when they are dealing with new and different people, places, and processes. Also, having things in order and following a sequence makes your in-person pre-trip briefing simple.

Here's what might be in a usual package:

- An introductory letter with *your* specific contact details where you can be reached at any time during the trip if they need help. This is always the first page!

- A copy of their overall day by day itinerary.

- Details of getting to the airport and any parking arrangements and the necessary timings.

- A paper copy of any airline e-tickets and reservations including seat assignment and luggage allowance rules for each separate air reservation that forms part of the trip.

- Copies of all hotel reservation confirmations with details of pricing and cancellation rules, local phone and other contact information and in most cases, maps of the hotels' locations.

- Any key local information and 'bumph' about unbooked local attractions.

- Copies of all BOOKED local tour and excursion reservations and details on how to join the tour, including maps.

- Give the travellers a 'Before You Go' sheet with information on things like mail stoppage, home security, newspaper stoppages, RX renewal heads-up, family pet concerns, passport validities and cell phone provider travel requirement. This should be a pretty standard sheet in each Advisor's computer.

- Travel insurance details and policy copies.

- Written information on government travel requirements for each destination such as visas, health considerations, and security.

- Include information on currency and exchange rates, weather and climate expectations for each destination. Some of this can be time sensitive.

- Include a copy of the Canadian Government 'Travel Report' for each country to be visited including details of embassy and consulate location and contacts.

- Give the client copies of a 'Leave Behind' list for clients to give to their family or friends detailing when and where they will be and how to contact them at each location, i.e., a hotel list and contact information at each stop.

- Finally give them a copy of their invoice(s) and a financial report of what they've spent and what they'll need to pay while travelling.

All of this should be generally in the order that they'll encounter while travelling. The document also is the aide-memoire for your briefing. That briefing should take up to an hour if you do it properly for a multi-destination custom designed trip.

All of this can be included in an e-document format, but I advocate that you should also provide a hard copy. There can be power outages and batteries do run down and people are susceptible to misplacing their phone or running into a number of other electronic problems. Both ways are best.

By the way, we found clients often kept these as mementoes and reminders of the trip itself!

15.
ON RETURN

HOPEFULLY ALL of your clients will eventually come home from any trip you arrange. Some may drop by your place to talk about the trip, but not many, as they don't have time for the face-to-face get-together or are just too busy getting on with life. Instead, you need to do a couple of things within a few days of their return. You need to call them on the phone and ask about the trip; what went wrong if anything, what could have been better and what went right. Don't shy away from asking about all three. Get the bad out of the way up front and finish off by reinforcing the positive.

Why do this, especially if you find it an uncomfortable task? You'll find it's far easier and less expensive to retain a customer now than it is to gain a new one later. Even if there were problems, the reasonable customer will know you care, whereas if there is no call, or just a computer-generated message, the customer would be justified in thinking you were afraid to ask or that you just don't care.

Some Advisors may be tempted to send a welcome home card, an email, a social media message, or text a message to the traveller on their return. Don't do that. Human contact is the best way to communicate as it proves to the client they are worth your time. The worst thing you can do is ignore them completely!

Once they have returned and you've followed up, stay in touch. Not daily, not weekly but about once every two or three months. Don't flood them with what in essence are advertising messages. Unless they are mega-rich, most people travel no more than two or three times a year. In today's world they are already inundated with advertising and promo messages. The rarest form (and therefore valuable) manner of communicating today is the old-fashioned letter that arrives in the post. A hand addressed envelope is almost guaranteed to be opened and read, they are that rare! Hell, it might be sold on the Antique Road Show some day. The note inside can be typed and you may want to avoid overt advertising pieces and focus on updates on your travel thoughts and some of the highlights of what you're doing. Invite replies. In essence, you become business friends through a series of personal letters. You can, and I think should, have a prepared set of notes and letters on travel subjects that can be crafted over time and will lead the client to look forward to the next one.

Over time this will build you a clientele who regard you as their personal Travel Advisor and will keep you well in front of any website that treats them as just another user. Remember, the strength of travel websites is lots of information. Your strengths are a human touch, personal judgment, knowledge, skill, understanding, expertise, comprehension, acumen, and discretion. Play to your strengths.

16.

YOU WILL SCREW UP – SO WHAT THEN?

NOBODY IS perfect, we're all human. Me, more than most. I'm the first to admit it! When a mistake happens, it happens. What you do about it is what matters.

We will all make mistakes; we will forget something and there will be consequences! What you do about it is vital to maintaining a long-term relation with a client. You need to do three things.

- **Acknowledge** the mistake/problem. Accept your responsibility, fully or partially as may be the case and let the client know you made a mistake. Don't be mealy mouthed about it, if you did it, say so.

- **Apologize** for what happened. Sincerely!

- **Act.** Tell the client what you will do to rectify the situation, if possible. Most people are reasonable.

At one point I had a senior Advisor (he'd been in the industry for more than two decades) really blow it! He had a long term client and his wife on a fourteen day Baltic cruise that was very expensive and he extensively briefed the client and provided him with a comprehensive document package and sent him on his way. A few weeks later the client returned to the office when the cruise ended and told the Advisor he had to seek medical attention in Copenhagen. I can't remember the ailment but he couldn't find a copy of his travel medical policy and could our guy find him a copy. He was in a hurry and would drop in tomorrow to pick up a copy of the policy. The Advisor (no names, no pack drill, it wasn't me, but I was the agency owner/manager) searched his records and the insurance company's website and finally realized that although the client had completed the questionnaire, the Advisor had forgotten to issue the policy. Now we were in trouble. The Advisor sat down using the completed questionnaire and worked out what the policy would have cost with the hope that it might offset some of the amount we would have to pay out to the client.

The client came back the next day and brought with him a copy of the clinic's invoice for the medical treatment he received in Copenhagen. It was for something in the order of CAD $750 after conversion to Canadian dollars. Thankfully he wasn't in the US! When the Advisor saw that, he let out a big but quiet sigh of relief. The cost of the insurance policy would have been over CAD $900. We made a deal with the client, who was very understanding. He would absorb the cost of the treatment and we wouldn't charge him for the policy. The Advisor did admit the mistake, apologized profusely, and thanked the client for his forbearance and understanding. If memory serves me right the client did come back at least once to arrange another cruise, just before we closed the business.

A couple of hints:

- Use a checklist of things to be done for each trip and use it to make sure all tasks have been completed.

- If you're an agency owner, make sure your agency's business insurance policy covers errors and omissions made by the agency or agents. You'll have fewer sleepless nights.

You will screw up. Do everything you can not to screw up, but if you do, treat the client honestly!

17.
GOOD, BETTER, BEST

TODAY'S TRAVEL agency business is much better at developing individual travel agents and Advisors than it was in the past. Previously, people entered the business right off the street and into the firing line. Now there seems to be a more clearly recognized path to employment in the industry, in parts of Canada at least. Storefront agencies may get a lot of their new blood from community college graduates. These tend to be younger, less experienced individuals. The emergence of 'host agencies' has led to more mature individuals entering the business from a variety of backgrounds, but with less of a formal travel education. Regardless of where people start, there seems to me to be a need for a recognized planned progression for front line people to advance their careers in an agency environment.

Once a person is hired to deal with the travelling public there are no 'spring training games'. Everything is live and the score starts from day one. Yet, the path for moving from rookie to good to better then best should be clearly established.

An individual coming in directly off the street to a host agency needs a fair bit of training even if they're experienced travellers. Not only do they need training on some basics, which the host agency provides (although much of it seems to be done through e-training), they should be assigned to an experienced agent/Advisor to ensure the clients' interests are always well served. This type of relationship should be formal and extend over a significant amount of time, at least a year. It may not involve all face to face time but should involve discussion of every file they handle in the first year.

For a storefront operation, the newbie should at least spend four to six months working at the direction of an experienced agent. After that they should have an ongoing relationship with their mentor until they've got a year under their belt. Regardless of the type of agency, they need to personally travel once or twice that first year. After that, regular travel should be part of their ongoing job training.

After the first year, a manager or experienced agent should be available for consultation and direction until they have a couple of years under their belt. Then they should be able to work without direct supervision if they continue to make progress. By then, their clients should be well served for any normal requirements. After they have two or three years under their belt, they should be able to advance their skills and knowledge to the level of a Travel Advisor. Additional courses in things like groups and exotics and complicated air should be part of their ongoing training. In some provinces there are legal requirements to be a manager but in truth that government stuff is pretty mickey-mouse. A real manager should be given the task of working with their people to ensure they are well trained and directed. The manager's job isn't to sell but to train, develop, and guide their agents and Advisors toward individual success and client satisfaction.

18.
EMOTIONS DECIDE!

I WANT to be careful here as we are Travel Advisors, not psychologists, but having a very basic understanding of how people make decisions may help you sell travel more successfully. There is an old saying in the 'sales' world that people 'decide emotionally and justify it logically' and there may be a lot of truth in the saying.

There are whole lists of emotions that can be generated such as:

- Amusement
- Pleasure
- Awe
- Contentment
- Desire
- Embarrassment
- Pain
- Relief
- Sympathy
- Boredom
- Confusion
- Interest
- Pride
- Shame

- Contempt
- Triumph.

Which ones will best help you frame a traveller's desire to travel?

Think of it this way. If you say something with an emotional content to a person, it will elicit an unconscious physical response from the body back to the person's brain. Either this response feels good or it feels bad, based on that person's prior experiences. It's a matter of pleasure or pain based on experience. If it's pleasurable the recipient will feel positive and the reverse is true. Of course, what you *say* isn't the only basis for making a decision, there will also be emotional reactions to you as a person, to the travel situation and a number of other factors, but it is a matter of having the odds on your side.

If in the early part of a discussion you ask a person what their worst travel experience was, their body is apt to signal pain to the person's mind and all could be lost! Not a good idea.

If on the other hand you ask them what their most pleasant trip was, their body's response will, in all likelihood make them feel positive. You should then carry on the conversation by asking them to expand on why it was such a successful trip and why they were so happy about it. Reinforce the good feelings being generated by that person. The client may then find the logic to justify the commitment to the suggested travel experience.

Help them enjoy the buying experience and your success in developing a longer-term client will be much more likely.

19.
WORDS COUNT

IN TODAY'S Instagram-obsessed world, words still count! You can come back from a trip with pictures but can you come back and have a story to tell? As an app, Instagram may work for images but as a story telling tool, it's pretty light.

There are over 170,000 words used in the English language and they have been used for centuries to tell travel stories. Digital photographs are a rather new technology. In the good old days (1960s and 70s), if you were meeting with a traveller and they offered you a chance to come to their place to see their 'slides' from a trip, most of you would have found a way to run in the opposite direction, fast.

Pictures can't make a case or argument for doing one thing over another. Pictures can't persuade people that one course is better than another. Pictures can't explain an idea or concept alone. Pictures are a support for all of these verbal activities but can't on their own, achieve what words might. Take good pictures. I've been trying to do it for decades for my own enjoyment of catching a vision at a particular moment. Better still, work at improving your verbal skills. You can inject an idea into another person's brain with words. Pictures help you illustrate a concept but photos on their own can't present ideas. If you're in the travel business you need to master the use of words, both verbally and in writing.

Like many things, the skillful use of words is a matter of practice and usage. When meeting with a client, the better you are at using words to explain and persuade a client of the benefit of what you're offering, the more successful you'll be at helping them to decide on their own course of action. Holding up a picture and not saying anything would just confuse a client. Words make a difference. The better you are at telling stories, explaining things, describing places and persuading people, the better you will be at helping your clients.

Two things will help you improve your skills in dealing with people and grow your travel business. Read a lot, particularly about travel and write a lot about travel. Start with guide books on places that interest you. Move on to fiction focused on travel destinations. Learn to discern in reading travel writing what is important and what is ephemeral. Read authors like Donna Leon about Venice, Peter Mayle about Provence, Henning Mankell about Sweden, Ferenc Mate about anywhere, Frances Mayes about Tuscany, Bill Bryson about anywhere but especially Australia and Rick Steves about Europe. There are thousands more if you want. Consider it professional development.

You should also put pen to paper or fingers to a keyboard. You need not share your practice efforts with others, but don't stop practicing. Writing helps not only to describe something else to another person but even more importantly it helps you organize your own thoughts. Writing is a skill that improves only with practice.

Words are the tools you'll need to help your clients travel well. Become a crafts-man; wield your tools with skill and care! Your success depends on it.

20.
PEOPLE TRAVELLING ON BUSINESS

I WAS a corporate road warrior in my younger years and I've been lucky enough to travel a lot for leisure reasons. As a travel agency owner and a Travel Advisor, I have never done or wanted to do corporate travel but I did have a number of people/clients who travelled for business reasons.

To me, corporate travellers are people travelling for business reasons and have their costs covered by the large/public corporation they work for. The corporate road warrior normally has to follow a set of rules and policies they have no control over, which are sometimes quite rigid. Corporate road warriors need to be cost conscious and need to fiddle the rules if they are to have fun! Most corporate travel agency services are provided by other large specialist agencies and consortiums that make that their main focus. From my perspective, it's best left to those types of operations. It's highly competitive and attracts lower margins and as I saw it, there wasn't a lot of room for creativity. You need to be a skilled reservationist who is highly competent in working with a reservation system and know international air fare rules and regulations in extreme detail.

'Business' travel on the other hand is usually for people who are self-employed or own small operations with some employees and who are controlling their own travel and end up paying the bill out of their own pocket in one way or another. Business travellers can have fun, and do, and spend as they see fit. The people I saw were doctors, dentists, lawyers, geologists and other independent business people and professionals. Some took their families with them. They took pleasure in combining business and leisure. They were also pretty relaxed and creative about what they wanted to do. They'd go to conferences, exhibitions, professional development sessions, client visits and business meetings. Comfort and reasonable costs were their main considerations. Creativity was valued by these types of people in many cases and they were open to suggestion. Some call this 'Bleisure' travel.

One thing anybody working on business travel should do is have a good world map readily available at all times as some of the places they'd end up in were pretty weird and wonderful spots. One time I had to arrange what was in effect an around-the-world trip for a gold geologist to very remote spots, from north Sweden to Papua New Guinea and a bunch of places in between. I think we used five or six airlines, a few of them of the low-cost variety (i.e., Lyon Air) to do a series of stops on different tickets and undercut an official round the world ticket substantially.

I'm prejudiced, but personal and small business and leisure travel is more fun!

21.
ME AND MY NEW FRIENDS!

WHILE I'VE helped arrange for hundreds of people to travel in groups, many of which I've had a big hand in designing, personally I'm not a big fan of that type of exploring. Left to my own devices, the only person I want to travel with is my wife and maybe my dog!

Being the group leader for more than my small family was always time consuming and hard work. Yes, it can be profitable and many people enjoy sharing their travels (see social media), but I'm not one of them. We like to do and see what we like and we always need to go at our own pace. We have easily wasted a whole afternoon in a Parisian café doing nothing more than talking, drinking wine and a lot of people watching. Not what I'd call a group activity.

If, as a Travel Advisor you enjoy group travel, good for you, but be prepared for a lot of work if you want it to be a success. You can end up with a lot of different tasks including group sponsor and head sales person, itinerary designer, chief accountant, complaint department and tour escort and guide. You'll end up with a number of new friends and maybe just a few foes! Your life will be filled with details, details and more details.

To make life a little less complicated and allow you time to do other business, can I make a couple of suggestions?

- If possible, find a sponsor or sponsoring organization that will promote and sell the group trip, to share the work load. You then only need to do the individual bookings.

- If possible (and maybe necessarily in some places), use a professional guide to escort the trip as they have the knowledge, experience, and qualifications to handle this part of the trip properly. For example, in Scotland you need to hire a Blue Badge Guide for group trips and while it has its costs, it is money well spent.

- Start small (groups under twenty people) before you decide to go big.

- Be clear up front on who's making what decisions.

- There's an old army saying that 'crap happens' so be prepared and do some thinking beforehand. As I've mentioned elsewhere, 9/11 happened and I had fifty dentists and some wives in Ireland and it was nothing you could prepare for! Worry about misconnections, lost baggage and cold rooms. Those are things you can sort out.

- If you have a group trip that is a success, repeat it next year. Hopefully you learned a lot the first time and it makes all the subsequent departures much easier to arrange.

- Design a lot of flexibility into your itinerary so you can adapt as circumstances change. Don't over program the group.

- If possible, let other agents and agencies who you trust sell into your group. You'll end up with a higher chance of success.

This type of travel can be profitable for any agency but you need to spend a lot of time on it and do it well. If you do, the people who travel with your group might well do some of their individual travel with you also. Good Luck.

22.
WHERE IN THE WORLD ARE YOU?

SOMEWHERE ALONG the line in school you may have taken a course in geography. Now is when it might start to pay off, if you paid attention to your teacher!

How much did you learn? Test yourself. Try these three questions:

- What countries share a common border with Ukraine?
- Can you use and understand maps and what they are telling you?
- Do you have a picture of the physical layout of the world in your head? You'll need it, especially if you want to speak authoritatively to well-educated, worldly clients.

Try this online quiz:

**https://www.worldatlas.com/quizzes/
geography-iq-test-how-much-do-you-know-the-world/1/**

However, there's much more to geography than basic political lineups of countries. As a Travel Advisor you need to know in some detail the basic physical geography of the world and the human geography of any area you plan to specialize in for your travel practice. Human geography relates to cultural, economic, health, history, transportation, politics, social organization and achievements.

For example, if you want to grow your travel practice to a place like France, you need to know a lot about that country. Where are the centres of French art, attractions, music, food and drink, design and writing? What are France's big businesses and economic achievements? What places do France's rail service and major highways connect to? How long does it take to get from place to place? What key aspects of French history do you need to understand? How healthy are the French? Who's in power, politically? What has the French nation achieved over the last 100 years? What are the political sub-divisions of the French state and why are they important to a traveller? Who are the key political figures in France currently? You'll need to collect reference material about your specialties. If you can answer or find the answers to most of these questions about France and have been there at least a couple of times, then you're on your way to being a specialist on France.

I doubt anybody could know the whole world this way. Some people may be able to accumulate this type of knowledge for a continent over a lifetime of work, but for most of us, we need to narrow our focus if we wish to specialize in a destination. There is no doubt you'll need to gain some of this knowledge even if you plan to specialize in a specific type of travel such as cruising. What's happening at the various port destinations that are called on by cruise ships? Why are they going there? Is it interesting enough for your clients? There are so many questions and a world full of answers. You even need a clear understanding of climate and weather. So much to learn, so little time to study.

Truly, it is a lifelong endeavour to understand the physical and human nature of our world and use that information to help your clients. You cannot afford to stop learning. Curiosity is your strongest ally. As a Travel Advisor you'll need to stay on top of what's happening in the world. With the internet's enormous capacity to hold information, it's much easier to research and learn about a place than it was thirty years ago. Stay on top of things and your clients will value your expertise.

23.
MAPS ARE YOUR FRIENDS!

I ADMIT it, I'm stuck on maps. There are two large wall maps in my office, one of Europe and another of Italy. On my book shelves there are at least twenty book style atlases and boxes of paper folding maps of various parts of the world, some country specific, some city specific and some a mix of other regional maps. Those are in addition to the globe sitting on a side table. Plus, we all have access to Google maps on our computers. I have a very new GPS in my car and my phone has access to maps. I first started to actually use maps when I joined the army and had to use them to lead convoys of fifteen to twenty vehicles all over the back country using paper maps that were up to ten years old. They were a form of puzzle for me. I can use and read topographical and aeronautical maps and about the only ones I haven't used much are nautical charts. I love maps.

Now that I've confessed my bias, I'd like to tell you why I'm that way. My brain was first exposed to a map about sixty years ago. I understand the strengths and weakness of each type I mentioned above. Each contains massive amounts of useful information if you know how to use one properly. Each type has its strengths and weaknesses. Some maps can be outdated or not kept current. For example, the street we live on does not appear on any map or GPS, including our brand-new top of the line GPS. The last time I was in a civilized part of Italy just east of Milan we went into a tunnel and lost our GPS signal. Right in the middle of the tunnel the road split and we needed to make a last second decision on which way to go. I'd studied a map before we left on this leg of the trip and I had a good mental picture of where we were headed and made a good guess as to which fork to take. Studying the map paid off.

Paper maps have many uses. Planning routes is one of them. Not only do they offer you a direct route, often they can offer alternative routes around potential traffic problems, less direct but scenic routes, and they can be folded out to show small alternative destinations you can't see on a small screen. A good map book usually comes with a detailed index and a selection of city and town plans that are easy to read.

A competent Travel Advisor should be able to explain any route and alternative to a client for a trip they're taking. You need a good map to do that. It'll show attractions, scenic stops, service centres and a lot of other useful information. So much so that many times, I've had to tell my clients no, they can't 'borrow' the map as I need it for my business. They need to buy their own! No one map is perfect, so I suggest you collect them yourself and use them to help your clients.

24.
WHAT WOULD SHE LIKE?

ANYBODY IN a travel agent/Advisor job is apt to run into some sort of Customer Relationship Management (CRM) software. Many of these computer tools will give you 'tombstone' information; name/address/phone/birthdays, etc. Most may tell you what a client did and account for the money they spent. Stupid marketers want this stuff so they can bug the client once every day with advertising email! Save us from marketers! Very few, if any can tell you what they might do in the future!

You probably know much more about the client than the computer will ever tell you. You may/can have the insight into what they like, what they don't like, who and what may influence their decisions and what they want to do in the future. That's because you *talked* to them and they told you things about themselves and their intentions. In the military world that's called intelligence; when you know the other side's 'intentions'. In this case, you're not spying, your intentions are pure. You want to be of service. You also know that those intentions can change! People change their minds.

The best value you can offer a client is a strong, friendly, business-oriented relationship. As a professional, you keep contact through a number of different media, through which an ongoing conversation, at a pace comfortable to you both, allows a free exchange of information. Have you ever taken a client to lunch without any specific intention other than bringing yourself up to date on how things are going for them? It certainly doesn't need to be swanky. For some, a sandwich at Timmy's would be nice. You may need to take the initiative and make the invitation and pick up the tab, even if your boss won't swallow the bill, but it may be worth it. Show some interest in them as a person, not just as a customer. A simple ten-day, mid-market cruise in a nice cabin for two can result in a commission cheque of up to $800 to $1,000. What's $45 for lunch if you can keep that type of business over ten to fifteen years?

To accomplish that you need to do some preparation and approach the task systematically so that you don't overdo things or conversely drop the ball. Keep a client notebook (paper or online) and a calendar so you don't go too frequently or too long without contact. Make notes of likes and dislikes, family situations and other information you'd like to have in order to serve them better. Unless you're booking large groups, keep it one-on-one as the client will like to be the sole focus off your attention. It's about them, not you, don't forget it!

25.
ITINERARY PLANNING FOR THE PRO

THIS SECTION is focused on custom designed itineraries for individuals and small groups (under ten people). There are lots of online sites that offer something along the lines of the '10 Best Hints on Planning Your Trip' for the 'do it yourselfers' and some of those ideas are pretty good. The problem is it's not that simple for a Travel Advisor. The big difference is they, the 'do it yourselfers', are doing it for themselves and the Travel Advisor is planning someone else's trip. A Travel Advisor needs to go through three or four steps at least:

- You want to interview the client and get their input and ideas of what they want to do.

- You then need to take their input together with your skills and ideas and create a trip plan.

- You then need to discuss the proposal with the client, and make adjustments as required.

- You need to book it and hope everything you suggested is still available at the right price.

Here are a few ideas you may find useful:

Start the planning as early as possible. Availability and price need to be there when you go to book so that you don't end up promising or offering something you can't deliver. You also need to let the client know that once you start booking, there is not much chance of making changes, especially last-minute ones without incurring additional cost, which could be significant.

You need to pace the trip with an interesting start and try to end the trip on a high note. That will depend on the destinations. In Italy, if I was doing the big three (Rome/Florence/Venice) for someone, I'd always end up in Venice. It is truly unique and best seen in the evening when the cruise passengers are back on their ships.

Throw in one or two stops that the client hadn't thought about that would add to the trip. They don't need to be overnights. It could be an interesting little village enroute for a few hours. For example, again in Italy, if they want to see Pisa and Florence, give them a three or four hour stop to wander around the town of Lucca, particularly if they're opera fans. The walled town and the music of Puccini are a nice surprise.

Try to get them to use different modes of travel. Cars are okay but somebody has to drive and navigation can be daunting. Use a train instead where everybody can relax. Sometimes a quick flight is better than a long drive.

Give them a break day with nothing programmed, if the trip is more than a week. They'll need a chance to catch their breath. Make it at a real nice hotel or B&B where they have a chance to be lazy. If they're the go-go types that always want to be moving, get them to a place where their morning run or bike ride is over a spectacular route!

If you think you can get away with it, plan a small surprise for them along the way. Book a special restaurant you know and tell them at the last minute. You're the destination specialist. Or, arrange a special activity with a local. See **www.toursbylocal.com** for ideas. All this supposes you've spent enough time with the client to know, really know, what they'd like. Good Luck!

26.
LANGUAGE SKILLS

IF YOU'RE reading this book, you already have all the basic language skills you need as a Travel Advisor.

It's more important to be able to talk to your clients than it is to the people at a particular destination. As my Italian friends would say; "Poiché è più importante poter parlare con i tuoi clienti di quanto non lo siano le persone in unadeterminata destinazione".

If you can speak Italian, or any other language, so much the better, but it's not necessary, even if you want to specialize in Italia! Google Translate is one tool I've used to help me when I need to communicate in writing with an Italian supplier. I have no Italian to speak of and my French is well below rudimentary. So what! All I really need is a command of the English language so that I have all the possible powers of explanation and persuasion when I'm trying to communicate with my clients.

There is no doubt that among many other things, a language barrier between a traveller and a local can cause difficulties. When you have a person travelling to a country where it will be a barrier, you can offer the client two or three different possible solutions to overcome the problem. They can take language lessons prior to departure if they are so enthused. I did it once but it didn't help much as there wasn't much chance to practice prior to departure. That was my fault and a decade or so ago. There are lots of online language learning programs. Today if you live in a big city like Toronto or Vancouver, I'd bet that somewhere there is someone who is running a local language school for travellers in any one of the many of the world's languages found in those cities. As an Advisor you might want to find out who those people are so as to refer your clients. The second solution is to have the travellers join a group departure where the tour conductor will handle most of the important conversations for the small group they should join. Finally, funds permitting, local bilingual guides and tour escorts can be found in most of the countries of the world. While English is a lingua franca it is not spoken by everybody. Be prepared wherever you go.

The better you speak your own language, the better results you will have in arranging and selling international travel. As I've said elsewhere in this publication, work on your spoken and written communications skills to be better able to help your clients understand their travels. By the way, I'm all in on supporting multilingual skills for Canadians. Not only will it help your communications it will help you understand the rest of the world.

27.
'FAM' (FAMILIARIZATION) TRIPS AND YOUR OWN TRAVEL

AH, THE good old days, (at least prior to 1994 and the Delta commission cut surprise) when airlines and suppliers made an effort to give you at least a decent discount or free trips so that you knew what you were selling. Mind you, in those days the paying passenger coughed up a lot more than they do now. Today many passengers are normally paying fares that are less than what an AD75 (a 75% agent discount on a full fare) ticket would have cost in the good old days! Even cruise lines are tight with the freebies! Still, if you're in the business it really does help if you've been to the destinations you will specialize in selling. In many cases, you'll have to finance most of your 'learning' travel from your own pocket book. It depends who you work for!

It has been the practice of some tour operators to offer some agents FAM tours so that they feel comfortable selling their packages (air/transfers/all-inclusive hotel stays). Some offer a significant discount and some may even offer it for free, but those are few and far between. Beyond that, very few offer these learning opportunities, particularly beyond the Caribbean/South markets. Some operators and tourist bureaus offer European or Asian tours to high producers, yet I think newbies also need some help if they are ever to become productive. A sales person needs to know the product before they can sell it effectively to others.

All that said and done you will need to travel if you want to specialize in a particular destination or type of travel. You'll need to plan and budget for it and if you're smart and lucky you'll have an agency owner or manager who will help with the costs. If you can, negotiate for it going in. It's your professional development.

If you become a specialist in a specific destination or region, you'll need to go there at least once every two to three years to stay current and in some cases even more often. You'll also need to invest in current resource materials to stay on top of hotels and attractions and local transportation options. At least buy guide books, they'll help you in dealing with specific destinations you haven't yet reached. Today there are many sources of information on destinations and other specific types of travel. There are magazines about destinations and countries (for Italy 'Italia' magazine out of the UK is one I feel is useful) and there are online resources that may prove to be reliable. Mind you, advice and information from some professional journalists or online amateurs can often be wrong.

All that said and done, you need to be aware that your responsibility is to your clients and not just the tour operators. In the past, your primary source of revenue was commissions and an agency's loyalty was always to the person who paid you. Now with the move to service fees and in some cases lower commission rates, you owe your clients something. Your help and advice are only as good as your own experience and research. Invest in yourself and get as much help and training as you can from your agency and your suppliers. Your clients depend on you to have the knowledge and background to help them travel successfully.

28.
MAKING NOTES

IF ONLY my memory was as good as I remember it to be! Try this scenario.

Meet with a client on the details of a fifteen-day land tour of Central Europe for forty-five minutes. As she leaves you take a call from another client on the details of a fourteen-day cruise out of Venice that he wants to book. When that's over, look at the three phone messages your colleague gives you, then take a call from a cruise line inviting you to an evening presentation on a new route; and you didn't take any notes? I'd guess and bet ninety out of 100 of you will screw up one of those items and disappoint someone. However, if you had taken even rudimentary notes of the key aspects of each interaction, I'd give you a far higher possibility of not messing it up.

I've seen that done by a travel agent who worked for me. I know I have a less than perfect memory, don't listen to my wife, she exaggerates how bad it is (I remember her birthday is 5 July 19XX!). However, when I'm at work I keep a notebook at hand and jot things down. For example, my notebook for August 2007 to August 2008 shows that on 7 December, 2007, Henry Minto called to arrange a refund on a car rental he didn't need! Yes, I'm a pack-rat when it comes to keeping notebooks.

For bookings, I also used large envelopes for big trip files so that I have everything in one place and I have one file with all the client's documents and info sheets in one place and I don't have to worry about any computer failures or corruptions. However, each to their own! Your agency may have a protocol for this type of thing. If lawsuits ever fly your lawyer will want to see your file.

I have my own shorthand for a lot of things and I freely use airport codes and other shorthand tricks for the notes to make them quick and easy. I also keep another small note book with what I call 'tombstone' information such as pass-words, bank account information and other stuff I don't want a hacker to get access to if something bad happens. Have you ever counted up the number of passwords you have for various booking websites and your reservation system? Maybe I'm a little paper oriented for today's world but it works for me. If you feel like keeping your notes in your work computer, so be it. It just means you'll need to go back to work to get something you need if it's the only place where it is. Phones are okay, but you have a hard time talking to somebody and at the same time looking up info you need. Do as you will but I'm keeping my notebooks.

In today's work world most of us suffer from cognitive overload, we try to remember more than our brain can hold and we often drop something from our memory that's important. However you want to organize yourself, feel free, but keep notes because if you don't, something will come back to bite you big time, just because you forgot. The client will not be happy.

More on this subject can be found in a book titled "The Organized Mind" by Daniel J. Levitin published by Penguin Canada Books in 2014. It's worth a read.

29.
MAKE TIME TO TALK

MOST OF us ignore advertising, most of the time! Most of us don't like to be preached to by a company! We want to talk with people we like and don't want to talk to people who pester us frequently. If you are a Travel Advisor, you like to talk with your clients. After all, you're there to help make their lives more enjoyable through travel.

These days there are so many one-way communication channels you can use that sometimes it's hard to recognize ones that work, let alone the ones that are best. These one-way channels are usually structured so you're talking about what you want, not what they want and need.

Travel agencies and businesses can:

- Advertise on radio and TV and the web.
- Advertise in local newspapers.
- Send emails.
- Send out a newsletter.
- Text from a phone.
- Use social media.
- Advertise through their website.

If you must as an agent advertise, don't advertise product, advertise yourself!

As much as agencies can spend money and make advertising efforts, clients can ignore the messages or worse, get upset with all the noise. As a Travel Advisor you may get some benefit from these but you'll get more reliable and consistent business from people who know you and from people who have been told that you do a good job. However, you need to talk with them on a regular basis. That doesn't mean frequently (i.e. once a week), it means consistent two way talk and in a manner they prefer and about what they need.

You need to make time to 'talk' *with* your clients, if for no other reason that they know you're still alive. You need to understand your greatest success will come from you being interested in them, meaning you want to listen. You'll need to find the time to do this, and for busy agents that's not easy. I would suggest that most of us are pretty tired near the end of the day, so that may be the time to make a call and chat with a long-time client. Two or three of these five-minute calls a day over a twenty work-day month means you end up talking to forty to sixty clients in a month if they all answer. Prepare a couple of different themed questions for each month that can get them started and use these to kick-off the conversation, but let them take you where they want to go. Even with a couple of hundred clients, you'd cover most of them at least two or three times a year.

By the way, the cost is nothing! There's no stress for you as you're not trying to sell something, and it's a positive way to end a day. Try it, you might like it.

30.
GETTING THINGS DONE

PERSONAL PRODUCTIVITY is always a subject for discussion when we talk about people working in an office environment. Many retail Travel Advisors usually work in a store front or office where they seem to have little control over what or who appears in front of them at any particular time during their work day. While it is doubtful an Advisor will ever have total control over their time, there are a number of things that you can do to give yourself some control over your productivity. Here are a few things that may help.

If there is one main phone number for the office, have one designated individual answer all calls for a particular time period (suggest a two-hour period each) and take messages or explain to clients that the Advisor that they want to speak to is with someone else. They can take a message to be returned during a specific period/time window, if possible. You'll need some office discipline to do this.

If possible, have your clients contact you in advance to make an appointment rather than just drop in unannounced. If you train them from the start you'll gain some control over your time. You can't see most other professionals now-a-days without an appointment, why should you be any different?

Do all your email work at one time, each morning and/or each afternoon. Never let emails interrupt your work on a specific file or project. Same goes for text messages. In fact, if you can, don't use text messages for business. People expect instant replies to texts and if you allow that to happen, you will never get anything done.

I strongly suggest you take a file as far as you can each time you do something to it. For example, if you are making a booking for a coach tour in Europe, you should not only make the booking, you also should complete the invoicing for it at the same time as the information is still fresh for you. You'll eventually need to do the invoice and if you put it off to later you just end up having to review the file and remind yourself of the details again. I was always a sinner in this manner and it cost me at times.

You need to work at controlling your own agenda. Build a practice of reserving time to do your work. I can hear all the multitaskers out there wailing about missing something important. Multitaskers think they can do two things at once. It has been proven over and over again your brain doesn't work that way. At best you switch back and forth between tasks quickly, but not so quickly that you don't lose the plot or you have misunderstandings and it's quite tiring and usually counterproductive. Don't take my word for it. Checkout Daniel J Levitin's "The Organized Mind", an expert in the field.

There's always more to do than the time to do it in. Work at being more efficient and you will find your work life way less stressful.

31.
THOSE 'GD' GLOBAL DISTRIBUTION SYSTEMS (GDS)!

SOME THINGS just 'grew like Topsy'! The Global Distribution Systems (GDS) used by Travel Advisors are some of those things. I first used the Worldspan system in 1994 and took my training in Salt Lake City on how to use the product to book cars, hotels, and airlines tickets. Today the system is part of the Travelport family of products that allow travel agents and websites to make bookings for anywhere in the world. I've also spent some time on Sabre. I must admit I've been a computer hater in the past! Even today I start most things with a pen and a piece of paper. Yes, I'm that old!

Because GDSs just grew in what may be called a haphazard manner they can be quite complicated to use, especially for some of us old fogies! Over time the integration of these systems with accounting packages and graphical user interfaces resulted in essentially a fill in the blanks approach rather than a series of command line designed input. I'm starting to talk like one of those computer guys again!

Like anything associated with these systems, it takes a while to become proficient in their use. Just about the time you reach that exalted level, they change things. Either the system is updated or the business switches systems. You need to relearn something all over again. Sorry, I'm barking again.

As a Travel Advisor your job is to stay current on this stuff, because if you do, you'll become more efficient in the use of the system. I do want to say that your efficiency in using the system means nothing to your client. What's important to the client is how well you plan and arrange their travel requirements, not how efficient you are using Sabre or it's like. However, as many Travel Advisors know, not all travel suppliers (car rentals/hotels/airlines) are available in the GDS. For example, many of the smaller family run hotels and farm/villa holiday resorts are not bookable in the GDS. Some airlines are not bookable, particularly the low-cost operators (Southwest, but coming soon in a limited manner, Ryanair and others). Not all cruise lines are there and many tour operators are limited in their use or found in less than a satisfactory manner in the GDS. Don't allow these difficulties to limit the use of these non-participants.

Computers are a tool in your productivity arsenal, but don't let them dictate what you book.

32.
AGENT TO ADVISOR

EARLY IN life I knew that beaches were pretty boring places for me. Offered an opportunity to go to the beach or play ball with my friends, it was a no brainer, I'd play ball! Some things interest some people and some people are interested in other stuff. I liked games and I was a poor swimmer. It was an easy decision. It's fun to be good at something. Nobody likes to struggle with something they're not good at or even interested in.

In the travel business there will be some activities or some places you're interested in and some you could take a permanent pass on. If you're interested in something or some place and you put a reasonable effort into learning about that area of interest, you're about half way to being a Travel Advisor.

There are two decisions to be made. The first is 'what you want to do' and the second is 'what you don't want to do'. It's pretty clear that you need to focus your efforts on a couple of clear goals and let the rest come or go as it may. If you have a focus you can spend your time and treasure on that and ignore the rest.

If your career in travel is going to be fulfilling and remunerative, pick something, or at most a couple of things you'll specialize in and do the bare necessity of others things to stay in the game. In my case, I was interested in aviation and European history, culture, food and art and didn't feel much interest in other places. For me, cruising does not get me too excited and I still haven't been to a beach resort! I have seen much of Western Europe and yet I still have places I want to see. I've worked around airports and airplanes much of the first half of my life and understand them to a much higher level than most civilians. I'm happy doing complicated air itineraries.

However, none of that stuff happened quickly. When I moved to Western Canada in my early 40s there was nothing to speak of in the air freight business in Victoria so, as air cargo and air passengers are often on the same aircraft, I switched from cargo to passenger and started a travel agency with the help of a few others. Was I any good at it the first couple of years? Marginally. However, I worked at it and spent my own money to take my wife and myself to Europe as frequently as we could afford. I was lucky in picking the right girl, she liked to travel too. After about five years of daily practice and working at keeping myself informed, I started to feel comfortable about helping people in my new specialties. It took a while but over time our business and reputation grew. We were somewhat lucky that we located our business close to an affluent neighbourhood and we had many experienced travellers use our services and we learned a lot from them.

I always thought it is better to use the term 'specialist', rather than 'expert'. I'll leave you to determine how you want to label yourself. To me 'specialist' means I focus on learning and doing something specific while labelling yourself as an 'expert' means you know more about it than most anyone else. A travel specialist should be in a continuous learning mode of studying, doing and exploring their areas of interest. Once you have the time in and the skill and knowledge in your area of specialty, you've earned the right to call yourself a Travel Advisor. Only your clients will know for sure!

33.
GOOD OLD DAYS

WHAT WE in the travel business called leisure travel (vis-à-vis corporate travel) was expected to be if not pleasurable, at least not totally uncomfortable, in the good old days! However, things change and today flying, for one thing, is not what it used to be. If you are of my generation you might remember the glamour of flying, not today's survival exercise. Then again, you also may remember things like paper tickets, traveller's cheques, pay phones and so much more.

In the agency world things were a little different also. For example, while handwriting a paper ticket could be a pain, it did offer a 'bit of flexibility'. Make a mistake, you could change or backdate things, at least up to Monday morning when you had to mail in the BSP (Billing and Settlement Plan) IATA report.

You could arrange for a meet and greet at the gate, so the client didn't need to carry their four suitcases out to the pickup point.

There were no extra fees for seat assignment or extra bags. Real meals were served on flights. Flights weren't so crowded. I remember once on a flight from Cleveland to Boston on US Air in the 1980s, I was one of three passengers on the flight. In total, not just business class! There were more crew members than passengers. I should also say I'm glad I wasn't a shareholder in that airline.

I won't say security was a joke but it was superficial to say the least. Some carriers even allowed smoking, not that that was pleasant for the non-smokers. Glad they did away with that.

There were taxi lineups at the airport so you could actually get to your destination without having to wait for your ride in someone's Uber vehicle to show up!

If you took photos, you only had to wait for a week for them to come back from the lab. You put them in a box and there they stayed. You didn't have to look at all the stuff taken by other amateurs on social media!

Agents could get AD50s and 75s (Agent Discounts) but only off full fare. I used a lot of those in the air freight business.

Many of the destinations you travelled to for leisure sure weren't as crowded as they are today. Getting lost in Venice was fun and you saw a lot of the real city. You did want a couple of extra pockets in your wallet for the foreign currency for each European country you were to visit. Today you only need a debit and credit card.

In the good old days, the doorman, concierge, or front desk clerk could help you in many ways. Today's budget property is lucky to have one person on the desk when you arrive at ten p.m.

In the good old days, there were no travel blogs or social media mavens bragging about how they scored a great place for next to nothing! That was your travel agent's job! Go ahead and try to guess what will be new in travel in 2040!

34.
WHY I TRAVEL

I RECENTLY read an article, titled "Why We Travel" by Paul Theroux, a celebrated travel writer, published in the NY Times back in 2011. I couldn't disagree with him more. The reasons I travel are all the opposite of his. He wanted to return home and report what he saw and what he went looking for and found, the most unsuccessful places in the world. He talked of places like Egypt, Libya, Afghanistan, Iraq, Pakistan and others in this article.

I'm interested in finding the most successful human places, places that exalt in having found or followed the road to success in living together. Paul must be an American crusader who wants to fix all the bad stuff. I'm a Canadian and want to experience and report on places that are exemplary examples of people who have found ways to live peacefully together. The sad truth is that many of the places I'm happy to see have a long history of failure and conflict and have finally decided to be happy. What is it they did to achieve this higher plain and how do they maintain their peace and in some cases serenity? They work their way through differences and contentiousness and maintain their peace. We generally call these places 'enlightened'.

So, you'll find me in Italy, France, Spain, the Netherlands, Germany, Switzerland, the UK, and the Scandinavian countries, plus others. Many of these places, in their times, have failed. They allowed wrong-headed elements to take them down a road to failure and paid the price. They have eventually recovered and in my lifetime have learned to succeed in letting their people lead a peaceful, productive life and pass on those qualities from generation to generation over the last seventy plus years in some cases. It's not always smooth, and they aren't immune to disagreement or misunderstanding. However, they find a way to work things out, without maiming or killing each other. They are all aware that no single individual has all the answers, regardless of how forceful he or she is.

I enjoy the opportunity to wander through the vineyards of Tuscan grapes, soon to be Chianti wines. I love to sit in a sidewalk café in Paris and watch the people stroll along the sidewalks. A Stockholm park at midsummer is worth the high cost of getting to this northern kingdom. A walk through the small Dutch town of Monnickendam makes you realize how the people have lived here peacefully since 1355 at least.

I like to learn and practice the habits of peaceful, contented people who have a reasonable consideration for their fellow citizens. I also find my fellow citizens are in most cases amiable to finding these types of solutions to their problems. If I find that successful example elsewhere and can bring it home with me, then I feel my travels have been fruitful and have taught me what to look for in my own place.

Why do you travel?

35.
LEGAL REMINDER

ONE THING many agents and Advisors sometimes forget is the travel business is all about contracts and the laws that govern them.

I'm no lawyer and I've never had to consult one about a client file, but almost everything we do with/for a client is committing them to a legal contract. Air tickets, hotel reservations, car rentals, cruises, and tours are all normally sold via contract (that we may call tickets) that you and the client have little or no ability to negotiate. In many/most cases, the contract may consider an agency a representative of the supplier for a particular transaction and not the travelling client. That's how our little industry started. Travel agencies were the **sales agents of a supplier** and the supplier paid us a commission for our work. Many of us forget that little consideration.

Yet, many of us consider the traveller our clients. How do you make it work both ways? You'll need to think about it! In point of fact you may want to have your agency put together a standard written agreement between the agency and the client for the consulting work you do for them and then have it reviewed by a legal representative to ensure it's enforceable, in your jurisdiction. This way everyone involved knows what they agreed to and what it means to them.

For example, you sell a cruise to one of your good clients and they have entered into a contract with the cruise line that probably shows another country (other than the US or Canada) as the jurisdiction to be used to settle any disputes. Does your client know which country and what the rules are for that jurisdiction? You can bet it was chosen because its laws favoured the cruise line, to say nothing of the expense to sue the line in some small little country half way around the world where their liability is limited and any award would be difficult to collect!

Not much you can do about it but you have a duty to let the client know at the very least that they should read the ticket!

For those that don't know, there are three provinces in Canada with laws governing the travel agency business; Ontario, British Columbia and Quebec. If you live in one of those three, or do business with clients there, you need to see if you need a licence to transact business with their residents. Even some US states have travel agent registration requirements. If you plan to do business there, you need to check out their requirements with a lawyer.

We are now way above my pay grade! If you have questions, talk to your legal people before you get too deep.

36.
GOING ON YOUR OWN

AFTER YOU'VE been in the industry a few years and you can consider yourself a Travel Advisor, you may want to think about going on your own versus working for someone else. There are a couple of ways of doing this, depending on the province you will be working in.

You can start your own full service, stand-alone agency. In three of the provinces in Canada, you need to go through a regulatory process that can be expensive, time consuming, slow and bureaucratic. We're talking about Ontario, British Columbia and Quebec. The rest do little to regulate the industry.

I've done it in both BC and Ontario and found in the long run it was maybe more problematic than it was worth it in the long run. It can be expensive, you need a fair bit of capital, you'll need to rent or buy a commercial location, hire staff, pay general business bills and get accreditation from various regulatory bodies and provide them with money and reports on an ever-increasing volume. The advantage is that you keep all the revenue. The disadvantage is you keep the headaches!

In fact, new to the business and the city, I started a new agency in Victoria, BC in September 1994, and Delta Airlines changed the rules of the game in December of that year by putting caps on air ticket commissions. They were soon followed by all the other carriers! We survived and, in many ways, thrived until we moved back to Ontario in 2008. We sold the business to an employee (really cheap!). After a bit of a sabbatical and a little time working as a branch manager for a national chain, I went and did it again in Ontario. It was no simpler and it turned out no less expensive. You'd have thought I'd have learned by then! Finally, I found something that I thought might work. I found a host agency that simplified the process and allowed me to focus on selling and consulting on travel.

As an experienced agent I joined a host agency that charged a small monthly fee and kept a reasonable percentage of the commission revenue. It basically allowed me to do as I liked and only insisted that I follow the rules and use their accounting program. It was okay and I stayed with them until I retired from the business. There are at least two significant operators in Ontario that I know of that run this type of program successfully. Check out Nexion Canada or The Travel Agent Next Door if you're interested in this approach.

If you're going to take any one of these approaches you need to know yourself fairly well. Are you a self-starter? Do you have a head for business and numbers or have a good accountant that doesn't cost an arm and a leg? Do you like to take the initiative? Are you comfortable getting out there and digging up contacts and customers and like doing it? Will you miss the comradery of having fellow agents to talk with and bounce ideas off of? Do you have the support of your family and loved ones?

The big advantage of doing it for yourself is that you have the flexibility of coming and going as you wish and to some degree controlling your work life, at least as much as your clients will allow. You're on your own. If something blows up, you'll have little help. For all that, I'd do it again.

SECTION C
TRAVELLING

1.
MY FIRST DAY IN EUROPE

AS IT is for many people, my first time overseas was quite memorable. For me it was in 1974, if my memory serves me well. I boarded an old B707 operated by the Canadian Armed Forces in Ottawa and took it to Brussels, after a stop in London. I still believe the pilot was an old fighter jock reassigned to flying a more sedate aircraft than he was used to. The seventy-degree bank he used to line up for the approach into Brussels is something better experienced in one of his old fighters where there is no room for passengers! Very few people on that full aircraft actually got sick and there was little genuine screaming.

Anyway, I was a very young and inexperienced logistics captain in my green uniform assigned to National Defense HQ in Ottawa, leading a small and extremely low-level delegation to AFCENT HQ's (Allied Forces Central Europe) for a movement conference dealing with getting troops and equipment to a NATO exercise in north Norway. The other two captains from Air Movements in Trenton were pretty old and grizzly. They were at least in their late 30s! They had done most of the prep work and would do much of the presentation at the meeting. They had separate travel arrangements.

After getting a cab from the Brussels airport to a small train station in what seemed to be the middle of nowhere, I found myself on an open and deserted platform with a closed stationhouse. I thought maybe the cabbie misunderstood where I wanted to go. There was nobody in sight except a short scruffy old fellow who approached me soon after I arrived. I thought he might have been looking for a handout. Boy was I wrong. Turns out, between my very limited French and his comparable English, I managed to understand that I was indeed at the right place for my train to Aachen and that he wanted to thank me for all that Canadian soldiers did to help his country during WW2. It kind of put a lot of things into a clearer perspective. Eventually the train arrived; he walked along with me to the right spot, opened the carriage door and pointed me in, and stayed around to wave goodbye.

I got off in Aachen, Germany and called the transport office in Brunssum for a pickup which took me to my hotel in the small Dutch town of Heerlen. Here I met up with the others attending the meeting. This included a Brit, a couple of Americans, a German, my fellow Canadians from Trenton and a Dutchman. We enjoyed a meeting of allies over a number of beers.

The meetings the next day went well, once our heads cleared, but the meeting with the little man from Belgium is still the strongest memory of the whole trip.

2.
CORNISH TREASURES

ONE OF the best trips we ever had was when we left London in a small car and drove out to the West Country for a week or so. Many of you may visit the United Kingdom over the next few years and those of you that have the time and inclination should get out of the big city and head out to experience the simple pleasures of the counties of Devon and Cornwall. Some of you will motor down to Penzance and Land's End to say that you've been to the southerly most part of England! Too bad if you don't make the time to stop into two of the nicest little villages the country has to offer; Mevagissey on the south coast of Cornwall and St. Ives on the north (now bigger than a village).

The village of Mevagissey, with its 2,000 souls, is on the coast between St. Austell and Falmouth and has one of the most picturesque harbours in all of England. It seems to be a bit of a secret that our English friends don't want to share. While many of them make a point of visiting this lovely little place, they don't seem to want strangers from the colonies to know about it. Rarely is it mentioned in tourist literature and rarer still is it included in the itinerary of escorted tours as there's not much room for forty passenger buses in the village. Nor is it easy to access if you have any significant physical limitations as the harbour is surrounded by steep hills that are easy to descend but not so easy the other way!

The town grew out of two villages named after a couple of Irish saints; St. Issey and St. Meva. The people made their livelihood from fishing and smuggling, the latter being the more profitable, in all likelihood. I can't swear on the current state of smuggling though. No doubt the break with Europe will mean more opportunity for the men of the night. It's worth a stop for a few hours.

While Mevagissey is missed by most off-shore visitors, St. Ives is slightly better known, particularly if you're interested in twentieth century art. Almost due north of Penzance on the Cornish coast of the Celtic Sea, St. Ives is now a popular holiday resort and home to an outpost of the Tate Gallery. Unlike Mevagissey, where having a car is pretty much a necessity, St. Ives can be reached from London by catching a train from Paddington to Penzance and transferring to the St. Ives line at the St. Erth station. It also has coach connections to London and other local towns.

St. Ives has the mildest winters and warmest summers in Britain. Because of that there are four beaches in the town to enjoy in the summer. I should also mention that there have been unsubstantiated sightings of sharks in the local waters. If the beach stop isn't what you want, you may then prefer the art scene. The BBC film "The Art of Cornwall" said that the St. Ives artists "went on to produce some of the most exhilarating art of the twentieth century". In 1993, the Tate Gallery opened a branch in the town that added momentum to the local scene. There are also a number of local festivals that may interest a visitor. The September Festival is the biggest and runs for 15 days and involves poetry, books, film, and art. If you head that way, I was going to point you to the Garrick Hotel for your stay. While not cheap it is just on the edge of town and has a magnificent view over the coast and great sunrises on a clear morning. While it was a number of years ago, we stayed there and it was a perfect place for a romantic stop while touring the Cornish sights. However, times change and the hotel was closed in January 2020 to be replaced by a senior's residence! You're on your own now, as that was our favourite.

There's more to England than just the capital. These two gems of Cornwall are well worth a stop.

3.
LONDON AGAIN? MAYBE!

MUCH IS made in the world of travel of the great cities. For France, you think Paris. For the US most think New York or LA. For Canada, visitors think Toronto or Vancouver. For England, there's London and no other. Yet, after our last visit, I'm not sure I want to go back to London.

First, you need to know that I've been there many times both on business and for pleasure. I've enjoyed the culture of the city and our ability to walk and wander all around or take a subway to a destination. In fact, on our first trip together my wife and I spent half our holiday in and about London.

On our last visit, about ten years ago now, we were there in October. We probably spent five or six days and visited some old favourites and tried to hit a couple of new places. However, there were two problems.

The first is it was extremely expensive. We're not rich nor are we paupers. The costs in the city drained us and we ended up paying too much for less than satisfactory accommodations and begrudged the cost of most other things including meals. Yes, we did go into Harrods but certainly left empty handed. I'll confess that we can be cheap, but it felt more like a survival show than enjoyable.

There was a second problem. We witnessed but didn't become participants in a relatively minor display of violence. We were having a quick evening meal in some North American branded cheap Italian place, about a half step above MacDonald's, when a table of five or six large local young men decided to do a dine and dash! The only problem for them was that the front door was double hung with the outside opening in and the inside also opening in. The dashers made it to the first door before the restaurant staff, all of whom were of 'Smurf' stature, arrived to give battle! After a general melee between the two sets of doors that lasted about 45 seconds, the bad guys got away and the Smurfs picked themselves up and dusted themselves off. At least one of the dashers made it outside without his shirt, naked above the waist on a cold October night. No sympathy from us. The Smurfs had a good all-around cry about having to personally pay for the lost money, and then went back to work. It wasn't pleasant to witness and it just added an edge to our concern about costs and the value of a trip into London.

We haven't been back since. Will we go back? Maybe, but high costs and violence did not attract us in any way.

4.

STOCKHOLM AND COPENHAGEN

I HAVE fond memories of travelling to these two cities when I was in the international air freight business a few decades ago. Due to resistance on the home front, I haven't been back since. She'd been there and done that and wasn't as entranced as I was. What I can say is that for me, the experience was always pleasant. The people I did business with were always friendly and commercially reasonable and they made the stops in their towns enjoyable.

The company I dealt with in Sweden, ASG AB, was a subsidiary of the Swedish Railway system and one of the larger international freight companies in that country at the time. It was later sold to a major Swiss competitor in 1999. My prime contact was a fellow named Christer Lafquist. I got to know Christer and his family fairly well and enjoyed any time we spent together, both in Stockholm and Toronto. One Sunday, Christer and his family took me to a beautiful restaurant in a hotel beside the sea in the town of Vaxholm (if my memory serves me well) between the airport and the city centre of Stockholm proper.

While the business work was interesting, I still got to see a bit of Stockholm including Gamla Stam, a walk through the Kungstadgarden on a beautiful June midsummer day and a meal at the restaurant that was part of Stockholm's Opera House. It was a very enjoyable afternoon. My favorite place to stay was the Scandic Park Hotel on Karlavagen across from a major park (Humlegarden). It was a gorgeous neighbourhood.

My travels on business also took me to Copenhagen, where I always looked forward to making a stop, although business between there and Canada was never a large part of our business volume. Our agents there were a company called Nordisk Transport and my contacts were two fellows, Ruben Olsen and Bjarne Laun. The highlight of one of my visits was an evening in Tivoli Gardens.

My prior impression of the place was that it was a children's playground full of rides and so forth, a Danish style Disneyland. However, that wasn't the case as Bjarne and Ruben showed me one night. We wandered around and had a very enjoyable meal and a few drinks in a place on the grounds that seemed to have no children whatsoever that evening. When I sat down to write this section, I noticed that my favourite hotel in Copenhagen, The Admiral Hotel was still going strong. It is housed in a converted eighteenth century warehouse neighbouring the Royal Palace and Royal Playhouse, alongside a historic dock in the downtown. One of the unique aspects of this very nice property was that some of the upper-floor rooms were built into the roof area and were two stories with a reception area on the main level and the bedroom above.

I must admit I'm still working on her to make another visit to the area. These Scandinavian cities are well worth a visit and each offers a different way of life that is very attractive.

5.
ONE OF THE WORLD'S BEST!

IN A small Scottish town in the shadow of Ben Nevis lies one of the world's best small hotels. A driving holiday a number of years back brought us to the town of Fort William in the Scottish Highlands on a day when, if you said it was "teeming out there" you'd be significantly understating things! A wet suit would have been more appropriate than the rain gear we were wearing. We were at the point where the peculiarities of Scottish B&Bs were starting to drag a bit and we wanted a little pampering. We had seen an article in one of the large US travel magazines about small world class hotels and noticed that there was a place called Inverlochy Castle right on our planned route for that autumn's holiday in Scotland. Thankfully, they had our reservation.

It's not often that we get a chance to experience a place like that but, when the opportunity presents itself, we try to grab it. Our normal travel style is to stay in clean comfortable and convenient local family run hotels that are not too hard on the pocket book. However, once each trip we try to spoil ourselves by staying somewhere a little up market…for us!

Out of the rain and after a smooth check-in, we were helped to our room by a porter who asked the magic question "can I get you anything?" After a few minutes the same young fellow knocked on the door with a massive tumbler of single malt that washed away all her road weariness from the last few days.

Our room was built around a windowed turret that allowed a 270-degree view of the…rain! No doubt on a clear day it would have been a magnificent view of the mountains, but alas it was not to be for our stay. It seemed that the rain never stopped once during the two days we were there and I have no doubt that even Noah would have found it a bit much. Back to the room. It was impressive in the extreme, with comfort and low-key elegance being the theme. No Trump glitz here thank you. A raised bedroom dais with heated bedding looked over a large lounge area and the bathroom was an enormous room awash in white tiles. The impeccable yet low-key service from the people staffing the hotel was as impressive as were the physical features of the property. The dinner we enjoyed in the Red Room restaurant was excellent and was highlighted further when we were directed to the drawing room for coffee and digestives on a most comfortable sofa facing a blazing fireplace.

While we only saw a bit of Fort William through a couple of quick breaks in the rain, the visit to Inverlochy Castle was well worth the time and money. For more details see **www.inverlochycastlehotel.com**. After our stay there it was back to Scottish B&B's!

For Inverlochy Castle, bring money and hope for sleeting rain to give you more time at the castle!

6.

IRELAND

IT'S BEEN a while since we were last in Ireland, but for various reasons much of it remains fresh in my mind. We've done a number of the main sites in the Republic (never been north) including Dublin, the Ring of Kerry but a few other things outdo those. As you'll read elsewhere, we were in the vicinity of Limerick with a bunch of Canadian dentists and their wives on the day 9/11 was happening. There's no doubt that took a little of the bloom off the rose, but there were other memorable moments during our two trips to the Emerald Isle.

The year prior, I think that our drive around the Dingle Peninsula was one of those highlights. There was a traffic jam that day, we got caught up in a crowd on the road, but no worries, they were sheep, and lots of them. When we did get clear, the way was one car (or two sheep) wide and while the surface was hard, I would never say it was paved! The day was glorious and the distant sea was as bright and blue as can be. It was just a good day to be alive. We stopped in the village of Dingle and wandered awhile then slowly made our way back to Killarney. It was a perfect day of doing nothing and seeing everything!

On our second trip, just a few days after 9/11, we did a day trip with the wives to the Bunratty Castle and Folk Park and I'd say it was interesting but the crowds were few and we had the place to ourselves. All the other visitors seemed to have gone home and ours didn't really have their hearts in it, they had other worries. The people manning the place were pleasant but I'm sure their hearts weren't in it either. It took an experience like that to remind us all how quickly things can change.

Don't bother with Blarney Castle. On our first visit to Ireland we found it more fun to spend the afternoon in a pub close by watching a bunch of Irishmen playing hurling on the TV and drinking Guinness. I still have no idea about the way the game is played. I do understand how to drink a Guinness, for all my Scottish heritage.

Finally, on our first visit to Ireland we planned a stop in Kilkenny so that we could visit my wife's ancestral home of Thomastown, just a dozen miles or so south of that big city. While her relatives come from Newfoundland, she knows that the Irish side arrived there from Thomastown, Ireland in the late 1840s. The graveyard is the resting place of a number of her people from that period. On the day we arrived in the little stonewalled lane between the ancient Church of the Assumption and the even more ancient graveyard, Kathy got out of the car, walked into the graveyard, turned left and almost sleep walked down a lane to a far-a-way plot almost at the other end of the yard and arrived directly at the plot of one of her ancestors. Just a little spooky as she'd never laid eyes on the place prior to that trip. Go to Ireland if you have the chance; you'll never know what you'll find.

7.
DUBLIN'S LITERARY PUB CRAWL

ON THE night before 9/11, we spent the evening with a group of dentists from around Western Canada who we were escorting around Ireland on the Dublin Literary Pub Crawl. We had done the tour the year before and thought it would be a great way for our group to mix and get to know one another. There's no better way to introduce people to three of Dublin's most convivial activities; beer drinking, theatre, and talking.

The pub, the poet, and the pint! In Dublin they seem to be inseparable. The public house is where writers sharpen their wit. This two-hour walking tour is led by a team of professional actors who follow in the footsteps of James Joyce, Samuel Becket, Oscar Wilde, Brendan Behan and many others. You will hear renditions of prose, verse, drama, and song from Dublin's literary hall of fame. The evening is packed with entertainment and also included a quiz with prizes for the winners. As one critic wrote, "A highly enjoyable evening that gives you the pleasant notion of replacing brain cells as you drown them."

Typically, the tour visits two or three pubs after starting in the Duke pub and there's just time between conversations to down a half of Guinness at each stop. While the drinking is done in the pubs, the performances are on the street. The professional performers are well rehearsed but there's no telling what some of the local street characters might add to the recitations!

The next time you end up in Dublin, give it a try. At the time of our trip, the cost was Euros 12 per person and it departs the Duke Pub (7 Duke Street, close by Grafton Street) at 7:30 p.m. most nights. Check out the details at **www.dublin-pubcrawl.com**.

By the way, don't do it the same night you arrive from North America, as the crawl ends about 9:30 p.m., but there's no telling what time your head will hit the pillow!

8.
PARIS

AS A general rule I'm not a fan of 'world-class big cities'. I've spent time in New York, London, Los Angeles, Chicago, Rome, Vancouver, Sydney, Miami, and Paris. I have visited all of them more than once. There are only two I would spend any more of my own money on for a return visit and those are Rome and Paris. Even with these two, I'm somewhat ambivalent!

Sharing Paris with the right person can be alluring. The core of Paris can be pleasantly walkable. It has a number of major places and establishments that beckon you in to see their treasures. This is an attractive attribute for a city. You can eat well. You can see the world go by as you sit at a café and enjoy a glass of wine with your companion. Whether it's a smoky basement jazz club or a sidewalk café, there is life that's not always in a hurry to get to the next thing. Paris and Rome are about enjoying life at any speed. That is the romance of these places.

For me one of the major attractions of Paris is its love and support of art! The Musée d'Orsay is the best railway station in the world. The trains are gone and the Impressionists are ensconced! To have a Paris Pass is to walk right by the long lines, then linger on the top floor with the works of Van Gogh, Rodin, or Manet; a perfect afternoon.

Le Jardin du Luxembourg behind the Palace of Luxembourg (where the French Senate meets) is a classic parterre garden filled with wide pathways, statues, pools, and people to be watched. It seems to be the Parisians' backyard in many ways. I clearly remember whiling away an afternoon with Kath on a park bench watching the locals and their kids enjoy the sun and heat of a summer afternoon.

If Giverny was Monet's home and the d'Orsay has some of his works, the Musee Marmottan Monet in the 16th arrondissement is the repository of the largest collections of his work and well worth the walk to the outer edges of the city to see.

If you must see one particular city square in Paris make it Place des Vosges, the oldest planned square in Paris. Located in the Marais district it was a place for the high and mighty to meet and chat up until the Revolution. Today, it is one of Paris' landmark sites.

On the other hand, having once been caught up in a riot on the Rue de Rivoli and having to climb the tall fence around Tuileries Gardens to escape made me long ago realize that it has excitements I can do without! While we laughed afterward, it reminded me I was in a big city and I must keep my eyes open. Recently security has become even more unsettling.

To see the rest of France conveniently, you need to go through the only big hub in the country and you need to be aware you're in a big city and all that means. Yes, I will go back to Paris as its benefits outweigh it costs, but it may be a while for me.

9.
PARTERRE AND POTAGERIE

THE LOIRE Valley has gone from being the playground of kings to castles and gardens for tourists and an important and proud agricultural and viniculture centre for France.

An hour or so on a TGV (Train a Grande Vitesse), a french high-speed train from Paris, will take you to the town of Tours, from where a rental car can take you to one of the more subtle but interesting areas of France. With my prejudice for small towns, we wandered off a few kilometres along the Loire River to the small town of Amboise, a place of 11,000 souls in the winter but probably triple that in the tourist season.

Amboise is a compact, but busy little town easily walkable and immensely interesting. We booked ahead and stayed at the now closed Le Vieux Manoir run by Gloria and Bob Belknap. They were attentive hosts who had a quiet old nunnery that had been converted to a charming, eighteenth century private estate and then a luxurious French bed and breakfast. That being said there are many attractive places in town to stay and eat. There was no shortage of wines to taste in the cellars!

During our short time there we visited three historic chateaux and left a number of others for another visit. The least interesting was Château de Chambord. While being the largest in the area it had the least stimulating interior and the grounds were large but unexciting. This 'hunting lodge' was a get-a-way for kings, as somewhere in its 426 rooms, he could get lost - with his latest paramour! Never really finished, it may be fascinating to history buffs but it is stark and relatively empty today.

The best and most romantic stop was Château Chenonceau on and across the River Cher. Here everything including the kitchen was as you would expect it to be in its heyday. Started in the 1500s, it grew over the years and passed through many families. Now in private hands, the building and gardens are a pleasure to visit and to wander through, for the roughly 800,000 people who visit each year, second only to Versailles. The gallery across the river is its most striking feature, but the place is well maintained and used for events, filming and has a restaurant on site. If you go, make a point of touring the multiple formal style gardens.

Within 500 metres of the Royal Château in Amboise is Clos Lucé, a small fifteenth century château, once a summer residence of the King of France. In 1516, King François 1st, a great patron of the arts, invited Leonardo da Vinci to come and work for him, offering him the Clos Lucé as a residence. Leonardo came here, bringing many of his works with him, including the Mona Lisa. This explains why its home today is Paris, not Italy. The château is well preserved, and today the building and the grounds serve as a Leonardo da Vinci museum.

Finally, we took time to visit the Château Royal Amboise, sitting high above the river and dominating the old town. An architectural jewel of the Renaissance, it is a UNESCO World Heritage site and home of the tomb of Leonardo da Vinci. This one can be visited in an hour or so and its proximity to the town centre makes it a place to see before dinner. If you are there at the right time, visit the town market and take a walk along the river.

This just touches on some of the attractions of one locale in this french fairytale region. It is full of the good things of french life. It's not to be missed.

10.
HOW TO SPEND A WEEK ON THE CÔTE D'AZUR

HERE ARE just a few ideas on how to spend a week as a visitor to the Côte D'Azur. I assume you'll be staying in a rented apartment in my preferred base, the old town of Antibes. Ditch the car and use local trains and buses to get around. You won't get lost, you won't have the stress of driving with the crazy locals (they are all part Italian), and you won't have the problem of trying to find a place to park a car and the cost of that parking spot.

- Day 1 – You arrive late today on a TGV from Paris, check in, do a little grocery shopping for tomorrow's breakfast and then find a place for dinner and a glass of wine.

- Day 2 – Spend the morning exploring the old walled town of Antibes. Visit the Cours Massena, the oldest and largest covered market on the Riviera. The antique/flea market keeps Place Nationale busy on Saturdays and the clothing market does the same for the streets around the Post Office on Thursdays. Stop for lunch at a local café and take some time in the afternoon to explore the yacht harbour and visit Fort Carré on the eastern edge of the harbour. If it's a typical hot late summer afternoon, head back to the local café for another glass of wine.

- Day 3 – Today is a good day to buy a One Day local train pass at the station and then head east. Spend time exploring the old town of Nice and wander along the Promenade des Anglais. This should kill a good part of the morning. Spend the afternoon in Monaco and bring money! If the Casino is your thing, bring money and a formal outfit. You can also visit the Cousteau Aquarium in the Old Town. Depending on your time, a stop at

Villa Ephrussi de Rothschild at St Jean Cap Ferrat (just east of the city) will allow you to visit their formal gardens and see the most palatial villa on a very rich coast. When the train gets you back to Antibes, have a drink at your newest favourite café!

- Day 4 – Today use another rail day pass and head west to Cannes, the Beverly Hills of the Riviera. Walk, shop, eat, see a movie and enjoy a little beach time. Again, bring money! When you get back, have a drink with your new friends at your café.

- Day 5 – Today wander around Cap d'Antibes, the luxurious neighbourhood on the west side of town. A long seaside walk is a great way to see the homes of the rich and infamous (to the French). Walk up the hill to the lighthouse and chapel and enjoy the spectacular views of the coast. Follow the Stations of the Cross down the path back to Antibes. Fall back into your chair at your new local café and have a drink with your friends.

- Day 6 – Two things today: Spend some beach time enjoying the sun and sand of the Riviera. There are three or four good places in the greater Antibes area for this. In the afternoon, visit the Picasso Museum set in the Château Grimaldi along the ocean side of the old walled town. By now they should be holding your chair for you when you arrive for a drink at your café. If you're in the mood this evening, check out Juan les Pins on the west side of the Cap d'Antibes for a little night life.

- Day 7 – Today is your open day. Do nothing or use it as the day to check out a couple of the inland towns in the area. Places like Eze, Vence, or St. Paul are all attractive and busy in high season. Let the local tourist office in Antibes show you how to get there. Don't even think of stopping anywhere but your place for the pre-dinner drink. Say goodbye to your café acquaintances when you leave.

- Day 8 – You're heading back to Paris today. Your TGV departs at noon! You'll be back.

You'd think I've done this before. It's okay. I'm going back too. It's a hard life but someone has to live it on the Riviera.

11.
PLANNING TRAVEL TO FRANCE, ITALY AND EUROPE

FOR TRAVELLERS, France and Italy are different than all the other countries in Europe. While most countries on the continent have at least one or two areas of top interests to visitors, these two countries may only have one or two areas that aren't of interest to visitors. In fact, in one survey by Travel & Leisure Magazine, between France and Italy, they had 17 of the top 25 attractions in Europe. Nobody else was close.

This concentration of cultural, historical and natural landmarks and sacred sites makes these places the most popular destinations in Europe. It also means for most people these countries are also the ones that attract the most returning visitors. I've been to both on multiple occasions and enjoyed each visit.

For those who want to explore in depth versus a quick survey, you'll want to plan your itineraries slightly differently. A visit to Portugal may involve a pass through the country from Porto to Lisbon to Faro in a week, then on to another destination, or home. A visit to France may concentrate on one region on a one week visit, then another area on a second visit and so forth. A week in Vaucluse, including Avignon, would not be hard to take. The next time you are in the country, you could stop in Gironde for the city and the wine of Bordeaux. As an aside, if you plan to stay in one place for a week or more, it may be better to rent an apartment or cottage for the whole time and travel out from there. It's more relaxed than a hotel and meal costs can be much less expensive and you'll have a reason to shop at the local market.

Another way to see Europe, particularly for first timers is to take the 'Great Cities' approach where you spend your time in two or three of the highest profile cities on the continent. The classics would be London, Paris, and Rome using trains and planes. Alternatively, you could do the classic Rome, Florence, and Venice, all by rail. The only problem with these approaches is that you miss most of what's in between! Personally, while I enjoy some of these large cities, I really like the small towns and villages in between.

I made the mistake once of deciding to visit the Amalfi Coast then drive up to Lake Como to meet friends. That was hard driving, taking about twelve hours. I also once went from Amboise in the Loire Valley to Antibes on the Cote d'Azur. Again, it was a long hard nine-hour drive. I don't recommend it to anyone. Until you have few restrictions on your time, you'll want to plan your visits to the continent in such a way that you can spend as little time on the road/rail/airplane as possible. Try to keep your visiting concentrated in one geographic area.

I've said to many of my clients "you can't do it all on one visit", it will still be there when you go back. Leave a little time to smell the roses!

12.
LAKE COMO

MOTHER NATURE made a number of beautiful places on earth and man has augmented some of them to a heavenly level. Lago di Como, or if you prefer, Lake Como, is one of those. A blue, deep lake surrounded by high hills in the south and stretching to the edge of the Swiss Alps on the north, it has become a playground for all types of people looking for a civilized get-a-way from the hectic pace of city living. The lake is shaped like an up-side-down 'Y' with the most memorable part right where the three legs come together. Here lie the villages of Bellagio, Varenna, and Tremezzo, all worth a visit but in my mind the loveliest is Varenna.

Having been there a number of times, Varenna is my personal favourite. In fact, we've celebrated at least two of my wife's milestone birthdays in Varenna. Small, quiet and hanging to the edge of hills that drop down to the side of the lake, Varenna in the summer becomes a veritable Eden. If you're lucky enough to score a reservation at the comfortable Albergo Milano for your stay, make sure you can get a room overlooking the lake. It's worth whatever it costs, if for nothing more than the view. It is, take my word on that!

The best time of the year is June, July, and August as the average temperature exceeds 25C. April, May, and September are a little cooler with averages around 20C. Much of the tourist infrastructure is closed from November to March.

Lake Como is not a secret. Writers from Mary Shelly, Mark Twain, Samuel Beckett, Hemmingway and Tom Wolfe have used the lake in their writing. Celebrities of all types vie for villas along the lake, with the Clooneys just being the most recent notables. Some of the villas, such as Villa d'Este open their gardens to the public. Some like Villa Serbelloni in Bellagio are now hotels.

An extended weekend is a perfect length of time to spend here during the summer. Take most of the first day exploring Varenna on the east side of the lake. No need to start early. After breakfast stroll the waterfront promenade, do a little window shopping and make a point of visiting the gardens at Villa Cipressi and check out Villa Monastero next door for their gardens. If you're feeling energetic, climb up to Castle Vezio, just above and behind the village for some of the most spectacular views of the lake. A late afternoon stop at a lakeside café for a glass of wine is a perfect cap to a day in Varenna. Supper however should be reserved at Albergo Milano, on their balcony dining room jutting over the shore. The view is superb and the food matches the view.

Start the second day of your stay in Bellagio first, checking out the boutiques, cafés, and their waterfront. Then catch a ferry to Villa Carlotta, near Tremezzo, to spend an afternoon wandering their Italian-style gardens and grounds. Find your own place to eat that evening and as you leave the next day, promise yourself that you'll come back. It's an easy promise to keep! No, I don't work for the Italian Tourist commission.

13.
AMALFI COAST

THE AMALFI Coast is one of the busiest vacation regions in all of Italy. This region south of Naples and for our purposes, includes Sorrento, Capri, and the south coast of the Sorrentine Peninsula, attracts about five million visitors each year. Generally considered one of Europe's most expensive destinations, a traveller can do it at a reasonable price if you stay in Sorrento and travel out from there. Having been there a number of times, this is what I would recommend to clients who were not in the need of luxury. A typical trip to this area can eat up a week of a vacation without much effort. There is much to do and see.

If you are a 'gazillionaire', you can stay in Positano, the second best town along the coast, in my opinion, and stay at Le Sirenuse, where the best available rate on their site for a July booking in 2020 is Euros 1,996 per night plus taxes and fees for a Standard Sea View Room! That's CAD $3,095 at the time of writing. In my 25 years as an agent I've only booked the property once! When we stayed in Positano we rented a three-bedroom apartment within a hundred yards of the beach, but we split the cost among five people, three friends from BC and the two of us from Ontario. While not cheap it was a great place and the per person cost was acceptable and well below Le Sirenuse. What I can recommend is lunch or dinner at Chez Black on the beach. While the food is good, the people watching is spectacular.

The time we were there we were having lunch when we heard a voice say "… hey John …". I looked over and there was another familiar face from our time in Victoria. You go half way around the world and run into people you know from home! Brian was there with his new girlfriend and as it happens not only did he know me but he was also acquainted with two of the other people with us. Small world!

The best kept secret for most North Americans is a village called Ravello. While Positano is tucked into a little sandy cove, Ravello is perched high above the sea on a cliff side overlooking the Tyrrhenian Sea just to the east and way above Amalfi. Well worth an afternoon's visit.

The view of the stage they set up each summer for the Ravello Festival of music is drop dead magnificent. The town has always been a destination for world renowned writers such as Truman Capote and Graham Greene and musicians such as Leonard Bernstein and Richard Wagner. There have been movies shot there and it is generally a retreat for the artistic types. If you have a little free cash (7 Euros) you can always wander the gardens of Villa Cimbrone. The gardens end at a lookout jutting over the sea lined with busts of various ancients.

The only warning I'll give about this gorgeous part of Italy is let someone else do the driving. The coast road is narrow, winding, and full of buses and Italian drivers and they all should be nicknamed 'death wish'! Hire a driver or if worse comes to worse, take the local buses. Your nerves will thank you.

Travel advisors don't get too many 'fun' movie-star moments during their working lives, but I've been lucky to have two of them and both in a similar manner at the same place, Ravello! On our first visit to Sorrento we decided to hire a car and driver to take us along the Amalfi Coast for the day as I wasn't excited about doing that drive. Too much work and not enough fun for me, the driver. So, at the appointed time Davide (pronounced 'Dah vid') pulled up in front of our hotel in a Mercedes S Class quasi-limo and off we went along the coast road. We made stops in Positano and Amalfi towns for a couple of hours each and then off to our final destination for the day, Ravello. Visitors must walk into the village through a tunnel from a drop off and turn around circle for cars and the local bus service. I don't know where 'Dah vid' hid while we were in town but as we emerged from the tunnel we found ourselves at the end of a lineup of forty or so tired, hot and weary travellers waiting for the next bus. Just at that point 'Dah vid' silently pulled up, slid out of the driver's seat, held open the rear door and we slipped onto a cool comfortable leather seat for the trip back to Sorrento! A gentle 'Elizabethan' wave to the gawking crowd and away we went!

On our most recent visit to Sorrento lightning struck, again! This time it was Tony, a senior gentleman who had retired from Princess Cruises and returned to Italy for a quiet retirement and to do a little driving to supplement his income. It was to be the same program as the last time, again ending with a stop in Ravello. This time things went a little off-side, as when it came time to leave Ravello we found Tony in an 'Italian' argument with a couple of female parking wardens who were telling him he needed to move his car. They were winning the argument but Tony had no choice as he couldn't get the Mercedes to start! After some discussion we all decided that it would be best for us to catch the next bus back down the hill and on to Sorrento while he tried to get the limo moving or towed. We paid up and wandered off to join the lineup at the bus stop. Just as the last bus of the day pulled in, up slides Tony in his slightly rough sounding Mercedes. He stopped; we hopped in the back of the car and made sure we waved to the others as we pulled away. We couldn't have planned it better. Travel can have its 'déjà vu' moments!

14.

FIVE LANDS

IF THERE is one place in Italy I would like to see again, it is the village of Vernazza, part of the Cinque Terra on the Ligurian coast. Multi-hued buildings surround a tiny protected harbour under the protection of an ancient abandoned fortress tower. It's a small place, weathered over the centuries and continuously adapting and flourishing since the eleventh century. Recently damaged by significant landslides and rebuilt by the locals with financial help from past visitors and fans of the village, this is a place with its own dolce vita! Their small fishing fleet will head out most mornings and be back in time for you to enjoy what they caught that evening, in a restaurant in the town square overlooking the boats tied up along the breakwater. Their anchovies, the mainstay of their catch, may be a bit of a surprise to you as they are nothing like you get around here on a pizza! They are large and fresh and without the salty finish you might be accustomed to at home. You should also know that pesto was born in this area and is a staple of their cuisine. Maybe it's because of the basil that I like the area so much. On a warm summer evening these foods and the fine local wines will make for an unforgettable and maybe a most romantic time.

You will probably need to climb as many as 100 steps to your lodgings as the tourist accommodations are primarily in the homes of the locals and they tend to be high above the square. The twin brothers who run a Sicilian style café called "Il Pirata delle Cinque Terre" near the station make the most amazing baked goods for breakfast. Think of it as a warm-up to your day's hike to Riomaggiore, the southernmost village on the coast.

The villages are all inside a National Park and you need a pass to hike in the Park. The first leg down to Corniglia is the second most challenging, after the hike to Monterosso. However, the views are splendid and there are plenty of places to stop and enjoy the scenery. The runs from Corniglia south are gentler but just as scenic. From there use your park pass to catch the local train back to Vernazza to be in time for dinner.

Save the hike to Monterosso for the next day as it is the busiest and the most strenuous. Again, the views are gorgeous, and since you will be working harder, you'll want the opportunity to stop, catch your breath and enjoy the view. Monterosso is the largest town on the coast and has many fine places to sleep, eat, and shop, to say nothing of its energetic beach scene, but it misses on the romantic factor infused into the life of Vernazza. Again, a train back to Vernazza when you're finished or a shuttle boat to enjoy a different view of this ancient land and another evening of eating under the stars before you call it a night. This is a land of simple pleasures produced by real people who wish to share their beautiful place with their guests. Enjoy!

15.

LILLIANO

AT SEVEN that September morning it was already warm. She was still asleep after a long and stressful day but I still opened the shutters to let some air into the room. It went from a dull, closed room to a bright sun-flooded stage overlooking a vista that only mother nature and man, working together, could have created. How lucky we were to be here, now.

Our luggage was in a far corner where we'd left everything piled up late the night before. We'd driven out of Killarney at four a.m., leaving our golfers behind, in order to catch a seven a.m. flight from Cork to London. We wasted a good part of the day at Stansted airport hanging around for our next flight and trying to follow the news. We finally touched down in Pisa, sometime around 9:30 p.m. and worried about how we would get there in the dark. The happiest part of that day was when we emerged from customs to find her two sisters and their guys waiting for us. They had been on the first flight from Toronto to Rome after they resumed. We hadn't any contact with them in the last two weeks and we weren't even sure that they had made it out of Toronto.

Everything went perfectly from there. We finally arrived in Lilliano after eleven p.m., road weary but content. We had made it. The night hid the farm but it wasn't important. Catching up, enjoying a few glasses of wine and enjoying the warm night air were the things that now needed our attention. We'd see the place the next day.

From my stage that morning, a movie-like world of long green covered vines hung over a sandy khaki coloured base stretched diagonally down to the farm's blue pond. The view was framed by two large urns of brilliant red geraniums. In the scene, three men in the distance worked among the vines, readying them for harvest. The cave we drove through the night before was revealed as nothing less than a half mile long driveway bordered by perfectly spaced, massive, green cedars. The house was quiet and it was a perfect peaceful interlude before the day started and before we started on the vacation portion of our trip. It felt like a dream, but it wasn't and isn't. It really exists. If you want to see the movie, click on the link shown here. The date, by the way was the 18th September, 2001, seven days past 9/11.

http://www.youtube.com/watch?v=X_ygVxRriyA

16.
GETTING READY FOR VENICE

ANTICIPATION IS always a part of travel. One of the ways we can tickle our sense of anticipation about a destination is to read up on the place. While guide books can give us information about a place, the things to see and do and the places to stay and eat, we want more. Tales of the people, what they are like and how they live are not often found in a guide book. For this you need another type of book.

Just recently I happened on a copy of John Berendt's non-fiction story of Venice entitled "The City of Falling Angels", published by Penguin Books in 2005. Berendt, an experienced author, has written a column for Esquire and was the editor of New York magazine. He's best known for his first book "Midnight in the Garden of Good and Evil" which was a finalist for the 1995 Pulitzer Prize. It was turned into a blockbuster movie with Clint Eastwood and did everything that any visitor starved tourist official could ever dream of for Savannah, Georgia.

Venice's Opera House, the Gran Teatro La Fenice, burned down in January 1996. This book is the story of what happened to the building and the resulting consequences of the fire. Even more, it is the frame Berendt uses to hang his story of the people of Venice and their foibles and follies. Here we meet the Rat Man of Treviso, Ludovico De Luigi, a surrealist artist and an agent provocateur, Archimede Seguso a master glass blower and Mario Moro; soldier, sailor, marine, fireman, policeman, airman, vaporetto conductor, electrician and much more!

The level of conspiracy described here owes nothing to Venice's ancestors and their politics and intrigue. The story of the fire, who set it and who arranged to have it set is woven through the whole book and is just one of a number of conspiracies that pop up during the story. Native or expatriate, none is spared. The sortied action of the players is awesome in detail and degree. Read the true story and you can pass on your next detective novel. The only problem here is that maybe, the mystery is never completely solved!

The story weaves around the arson and what it meant to the people of Venice. Berendt explores the various strata of La Serenissima's society, its moods and the melodrama that Venetians create as part of their daily routine. If you're to be in Venice in the near future it will give you an interesting insight to all those people who live in this most intriguing city.

Read the book. Then plan your time in Venice.

17.
MILAN – ITALY AT WORK

MILANO IS not your typical tourist destination. It's a working city of 1.4 million people and the hub of transportation, business, and economics for northern Italy. As someone else once said, it has as many banks as churches! That doesn't mean it's not worth a visit, but it wouldn't be on most people's list of destinations for their first time in Italy. Having been there (a long time ago), I have to agree. Yet, there are a number of highlights that make it worth a stop for a day or so.

Da Vinci's fresco, The Last Supper, in the dining room of the Dominican monks in the church of Santa Maria della Grazie was reopened about twenty years ago after spending a couple of decades being restored. You'll need to book this stop in advance as the number of people allowed to view this very fragile work is tightly controlled. Your stay may be limited to fifteen minutes.

If you're a fan of Italian opera, then a stop at La Scala is a must. For most opera lovers this is almost their equivalent of a visit to St. Peter's in Rome! It is one of, if not the largest opera houses in the world, having opened in 1778. There is usually something happening every night. However, you'll need to get tickets well in advance. Organized tours of the stage and its various collections are operated during the day and are a lot easier to book.

If you're a soccer fan, then a visit to Stadio San Siro, the home of AC Milano is a must. Up to 80,000 people can watch them play a home game here. You can also join a tour of the stadium and its museum which is open daily.

Milan is also the home of high-end fashion shopping so a stop at Galleria Vittorio Emanuele II may be a must do! This mall was opened in 1877 and hasn't looked back. It connects the Duomo at one end to La Scala at the other end. The iron and glass roof lets the sun shine in on some of the world's most highly sought after clothing. It's also seems to be Milan's preferred get-together and dining destination. Ask a local how you can improve your good luck under the main dome.

The other main shopping district for the very style conscience Milanese and their visitors is the neighbourhood called "the Quadrilatero d'Oro". This fashion destination is bounded by Via Manzoni, Via della Spiga and Via Montenapoleone. Expect to find shops for all the high-end fashion houses. No outlets here. Bring money and lots of it. Window shopping is a much less expensive option!

If churches are your thing, the Duomo of Milan and its piazza and museum are also worth the stop. It took six centuries to build this church and it is now number two in size to the Vatican in Italy. Try the roof-walk about 300 feet above the Piazza below.

A couple of other places deserve a mention. The Brera Museum houses a good collection of Italian art with works by Mantegna, Raphael, Caravaggio and Pierodella Francesca. Sforza Castle was once the home of the great Dukes of Milan and now houses an art museum and has one of Michelangelo's final pieces, his Rondanini Pieta.

Milan has two airports: Malpensa to the northwest of the city and its main international gateway, and Milan Linate, its main domestic airport just to the south of the downtown area. If you want to see both the south of the country and the northern areas you can go into Milan and home from Rome or vice versa. That way a couple of nights in Milan can be added to any trip.

18.
NEXT YEAR IN ITALY

IF I was travelling to Italy next year it would be in the late summer or early fall, but where would I go?

I can't remember how many times I've been there in the last twenty years plus, but I'd guess around ten times and each was for at least ten days. I've been lucky enough to see and enjoy a lot of the country and in some cases I wouldn't mind a repeat visit to some of the places I've been. More importantly, where new would I go and why? I must point out that these are my ideas and they haven't been discussed with Kathy and she would have a big say in what we do. At this time we have no plans, discussed or made, so treat this as a wish list. I suspect we'd want about two weeks all in to make this happen.

Here are some thoughts:

Sicily – I've had at least a couple of friends who've been that way and they all rave about the experience. While Palermo would be one of the stops, I'd really like to see Mount Etna and the whole east and south coasts of the island. If we did the trip in the timeframe I mentioned above, it shouldn't be too hot nor likely is it to be cold!

Turin – At the other end of the country this city is part of their industrial heartland (think Fiat) but it is supposed to be a city of art and culture, chocolate, and the home of a royal residence. This is in all probability a two night/one day destination for us.

Milan – It's been a long while since I've done more than drive through or around this commercial heart of the country. Again, I think I could do all I want to in just a couple of days here. The must do for me would be the Last Supper.

Lake Como – A long weekend here would be like being back in heaven! I might combine it with a visit to Lake Maggiore to visit Isola Bella and its gardens across from Stresa.

Padua and Verona – On the way south we might take a day for each of these interesting cities.

Bologna –Just north of Tuscany in Emilia-Romagna, the centre of Italy's biggest agricultural region and on the left side of politics, Bologna is most renowned for its food. It's not called the La Grassa (the Fat One) for no reason.

Toscana – If we had anytime left over, I'd want to spend it to the south and east of Siena near the towns of Pienza, Montepulciano and San Quirico d'Orcia.

My bet is that we could hit all these places by rail except Sicily, where a cheap flight and a rental car would work best. I wonder if I could convince her that it might be interesting.

19.
VISITING ITALIAN GARDENS

FOR MOST travellers a visit to a garden during your wandering is usually a relaxing delight. In Italy this can be done in many parts of the country. I spent fifteen years in Victoria, BC, and it is a city of gardens and gardeners and it was one of the things I liked about the place. A stop with an out-of-towner to Butchart Gardens, Abkhazi or to Hatley Park was always a success.

The same applies to Italy. There are different styles of gardens but they are always enjoyable if you're of that mindset. You can arrange your travels so that you can get a garden hit in most parts of the country and can arrange a whole itinerary around Italian gardens.

Working from north to south, there are a whole series of places where a stop would be rewarding.

Starting in the north, you could follow this route:

On Lake Maggiore there is the crazy island of Isla Bella, just off Stresa, in the lake, which is wholly occupied by the villa and gardens that form Borromean estates. Only money and determination could have created something like this island garden and palace.

Also, on Lake Maggiore is Villa Taranto and its botanic gardens, a relatively new development as far as Italian gardens grow, having been started in 1931 by a Scot and opened to the world in 1952. It has more than seven km of paths among collections of azaleas and 300 types of dahlias.

If then you go to Lake Como there are a number of gardens worth visiting including Villa Carlotta and Villa Serbelloni, Villa Melzi d Eril and Villa Monastero in

Varenna. I've seen three of them and they make a stay in Varenna a must do for even the most jaded of traveller.

Further to the south are Verona and the Giardino Giusti. Near the city centre this Renaissance villa and garden is well worth the visit if for no other reason that it has a maze that can challenge the most dedicated explorers and puzzle solvers.

Next is Florence and its Medici creations that are still going strong today, including the Boboli Gardens and Villa Gamberaia in Settignamo. These require a reservation. For a more recently designed garden, visit La Foce in Tuscany, in the Val d'Orcia outside Montepulciano. This is the estate with the winding road bordered by cedar trees that is the trademark of Tuscan vineyards and estates.

From there head to Rome and Villa D'Este just outside the city in Tivoli. The fountains and gardens are amazing considering a Cardinal built them on a hillside over four hundred years ago for the glory of God and himself! His ambitions to be a powerful pope were the driving force in building this place.

Finally, if you're going to be near Naples, make a point of stopping off at Palazzo Reale in Caserta to the north east of Naples. This is Italy's Versailles, both in scope and grandeur!

There are many more for those who enjoy these wonderful spots. You can also check out Monty Don's four-part series he made for the BBC on this subject. They are all available on YouTube.

20.
DRIVING IN ITALY

BEEN THERE, done that and have the scars to prove it! Everyone has their top ten list of how to drive in Italy. I have only one rule: close your eyes and pray! Okay, that might be pushing it some, but pay attention to the prayer bit.

Actually, it doesn't need to be that much fun but there are a couple of simple rules you can follow that might make your life less stressful:

- Don't drive in big cities like Rome, Milano or Naples. Just don't do it. As I've said elsewhere, take a cab, train, bus or rickshaw (if you can find one) but let someone else do the driving. You don't need the stress and you won't want to pay for the parking charges either.

- Some/many cities such as Florence have ZTL (Limited Traffic) zones that forbid non-residents from bringing cars into the downtown core area. Your hotel won't tell you that, but the cameras they use will tell the police, if you do.

- Realize that the motorways aren't for getting from place to place; they are actually there for the Italian's to practice for their local Grand Prix! They need to see how close they can draft you so that they can get past when a couple of inches open up in front of you.

- Italian towns and villages are very old and the local byways were there to let two donkeys pass. Your SUV won't make it. Rent a small car!

- If you're on a motorway, don't stay in the left lane. It's supposed to be for passing only. Remember this is the land of the Mafia and the lupara! Don't aggravate the locals.

- They use photo-radar and the rental car company has your credit card details. Enough said!

- As someone else said, familiarize yourself with the local rules and regulations, then forget them completely, everybody around you already has!

- Make sure you have a GPS, but it will lead you astray just about the time you need it. Paper maps will also be more useful in finding all the back roads you'll need to keep away from the locals.

- Get an International Drivers Permit before you leave home. You shouldn't need it, but the constabulary may be more under-standing if they can read it, when they stop and ask you for it.

- Always get the extra insurance. You think that rental car companies are nasty here about damages. They're not even in the competition.

- Realize that no matter how fast you go it will still take you eleven hours to drive from Naples to Lake Como. It's not a matter of the speed you go, it's a factor off how long you wait in line as they clear another accident on the motorway.

I bet you think I'm overstating my case! None the less, those are my eleven rules for driving in Italy. Pick your ten favourites and hope for the best.

21.
"CIAO" ROMA AND "ARRIVEDERCI"!

HAVING BEEN to Rome a number of times and usually arriving at Fiumicino Airport from overseas, I could see why you might be left wondering why all the fuss? Out by the sea, it is not the loveliest landing ground for a city of three million people. While there are a number of alternate ways into the heart of the ancient city, I almost always take a cab or a limo into the city. The train to Termi station is cheaper but always crowded and you will still have a way to go to get to your destination. Why waste time when you have so much to see and do when you get there.

I can imagine the shear confusion that a first timer would have trying to decide where to start. You won't see all of it on your first visit. Cover the highlights then leave time for three otherwise secondary but fabulous things to see. Yes, get to the Vatican and its museum; see the Trevi Fountain and then visit the Coliseum. Once you've done that and any other specific stops, try these attractions:

- Take a half day tour out to **Villa d'Este** in Tivoli (on the eastern edge of the city) for the gardens created by a Cardinal who wanted to impress his fellow Cardinals with his wealth and desire to be pope. The villa itself, while mildly interesting, plays second fiddle to the gardens which are spectacular. Bring your camera. This and a stop at the ruins of Villa Adriana will fill an afternoon.

- Back out near the airport is **Ostia Antica**. Less well known than Pompeii but in many ways better preserved (no volcano troubles), it is the old sea port of Rome. Easily reached by local train from the city, it's well worth a visit and will help you understand how the old city developed. A well preserved yet little visited relative to other Roman attractions; it is worth your time. If you want to stay in the area, try the local Park Hotel.

- The third thing to do is spend an afternoon in the **Piazza Navona**. This oblong plaza is the site of an old Roman stadium from the first century. Now Baroque in style, this highly ornate public space is filled on all four sides by the odd church and a fair sprinkling of cafés, bars, and restaurants. It is a gathering place for people from all over the city and beyond. The three main fountains are the secondary attractions. The first is the people wandering through this huge space. I have spent a couple of afternoons in one of the outdoor cafés with my girl, talking and drinking the odd beer and people watching. Try it and you might like it as much as I did.

So, "ciao" is the informal Italian for both hello and goodbye. Definitely use "ciao" when you arrive in Rome. "Arrivederci" is the Italian for "until we meet again". You'll only be gone temporarily.

22.
THE ITALIAN DAILY RHYTHM

IF YOU spend any time in any smaller Italian towns and some cities, you will find that the daily routine isn't quite what you are used to at home. No doubt the pace is slower than that in big cities and especially so in the summer.

Riposo is the time for an afternoon nap! It's a serious traditional practice of taking time for a break from work and for spending time with family or to rest. Many stores may take an afternoon off. It can start any time after noon and ends about four p.m. Sundays are still a day of rest and you won't find much happening or open. For visitors, it's a great time to linger over a glass of wine or find a park bench where you can watch the world go by, at least those not taking Riposo.

Morning is an active time. Stores are open and people are moving around and the retired folks are out for their morning coffee and conversation. A lot of shopping happens in the morning and even Saturday morning can be a busy market day.

Lunch in Italy is not a hurried thing. No dining and dashing here. A leisurely lunch in itself can help you get into the mindset for a sleepy afternoon nap. In all probability, anything you might want to do on a hot Italian afternoon may be closed and you'll need to come back later. Take a tourist tour or wander on your own. Tourist towns like Amalfi and others may still be busy but a village or small town may feel like it's shut down.

Small towns can be quite quiet. It's a good time to take a few photos without people, but lots of shadows in them. It's also a time for a slow measured stroll with no worry about dodging crowds, like it will be in the early evening. Many gardens and public parks will be open and you can have a chance to make a park bench a nice spot for a short shut-eye rest. Otherwise find a local bar and enjoy a drink and a chat with one of the inhabitants.

Early evening may be the most colourful time of the day as Italians take the practice of evening "la passeggiata" seriously. It's an evening stroll or promenade where they want to see and be seen with their neighbours and maybe enjoy a convivial conversation. It can be the busiest time of the day for locals and tourists alike to meet and greet. After that, dinner can go to all hours.

Regardless, as a tourist when planning your sightseeing, make sure things will be open when you plan to be there. Churches, museums, and galleries can all be closed on a hot summer afternoon. Beware that many places also close Mondays to give their people a couple of days off.

Adjust your pace in Italian small cities and towns. Adapt to their rhythms and go with the flow. After all, you're on holidays, there's no hurry and you can always come back if you missed something.

23.
MY MADRID

AS PART of our last trip to Europe we made a couple of stops in Spain, in late August. Our problem was we did not have much time, as it was to be a two-country trip, both Spain and Italy. Each only got six or seven days. So, we split our time in Spain between Madrid and Andalusia, beginning with Madrid.

Most travellers' memories of a city come from the specific experiences of things they did when they visited, and I'm no different. Yes, we see things, hear things, taste things but what stands out and stays with us are these personal experiences. What happens to us while we are there stays with us!

For me it was a night forage through some of Madrid's better hidden tapas bars. We joined James Fraser, the founder of Adventurous Appetites, along with seven or eight others, strangers to us at the time, for visits to four of his favorite tapas places one night in August a few years ago. Beer and morsels of different types of tapas from different bars around the centre of Madrid led to a convivial evening never to be forgotten. Yes, a few new temporary friends were made, lives were discussed, food was eaten and beer and wine were consumed in significant quantities. Seafood, various vegetable concoctions, jamon and numerous other tasty bits filled the evening along with numerous personal stories, some true, some positively not. James paced things out perfectly and was a gracious host. The evening finally ended well after midnight and we headed for home on foot with too full bellies and a pleasant bit of buzz. Then one of the biggest surprises of the visit hit us. There were masses of people, young, old and children, strolling the streets at two a.m. In fact, by my estimate there were more people on the street then, than at two p.m. that afternoon. So it is true, the Spanish have a different biological clock than the rest of us! I had heard this, but it is still a surprise to experience a major world class city living to such a different rhythm!

I purposely left off the names of the bars for two reasons. First, they are James' 'secret sauce' and he makes a living out of that information, so you'll need to do his tour to find out. Find him at **www.adventurousappetites.com**. Second, I couldn't remember them, even the next morning!

My other surprising takeaway from Madrid was El Rastro, the Madrid Sunday flea market. Every Sunday for about the last 280 years there has been an open-air market south of Sol that attracts 3,000 or so vendors and hundreds of thousands of Madrilenos. Even if you buy nothing it's more interesting than anything else you'll find to do in Madrid on a Sunday morning. Good luck and take care of your wallet in these types of crowds.

If you have a chance, make a stop in Madrid on your next trip to Europe. You won't be disappointed.

24.

ANDALUSIA

ANDALUSIA IS the autonomous southwestern region of Spain. While there, we centered ourselves in Seville and where time allowed, branched out from that home base. We treated ourselves on this stop and booked into the Hotel Colon Gran Melia in downtown Seville. This five-star property lived up to its reputation and the stay was quite enjoyable and for the most part, it allowed us to walk to anywhere we wanted to go in Seville. As we stated above, the Spanish live on a different timetable than we do. Lunch may start at one or two p.m. but dinner isn't really ready until ten p.m. Having been to Madrid first, we were starting to get used to things.

For us, Seville was even more enjoyable than Madrid and it was certainly worth more time than the three days we were able to give it. First and foremost, it's a walking city. The obvious visitor highlights are the Alcázar and its gardens, its Cathedral, the Barrio de Santa Cruz and the Plaza de Espana and its surrounding parks. For nightlife and places to eat, head across the river to the Tirana neighbourhood, but get there before ten p.m. You can have any restaurant to yourself if you sit down at eight p.m., but you won't find an empty seat after ten p.m. It's not just busy with couples and students. Extended families of fifteen including many children under five were still wandering around at midnight. The highlight for me in Seville was the palace at the site of an old Moorish fortress or as it was known then, and still is today, the Alcázar. While it looks and has been designed that way, as a Moorish palace, it is actually a construct of a Christian king who had it built (by Moorish craftsmen) over 100 years after the city was reconquered. The combination of buildings and grounds is quite fabulous and worth at least a three-hour visit, not including a stop for a coffee along the way. The building is interesting but the gardens were close to Paradise! The place is still a palace and is used by the current Spanish royals while they're in town.

While we were in Seville, we day tripped to Granada to see the Alhambra. It was a three-hour bus ride from Seville and then another back and if I was to do it again I would at least overnight in Granada. The visit to the Alhambra was worthwhile but as we did it with 3,000 other people at the same time, it was crowded and uncomfortable. I would like to see it again when there were fewer people. Some of the allure was lost in the crowds. We did get a chance to visit downtown Granada and enjoyed the chance to have a glimpse around the old town. One civilized practice they have in Grenadian bars and pubs is that they will feed you small plates of food for free if you order a drink. With each drink a new small plate of food. A most enjoyable lunch and the best way to prepare for a three-hour bus ride back to Seville.

There's no doubt this part of Spain needs another visit!

25.
AUSSIE SOJOURN

I'VE MADE one journey to Australia, and while there are parts of it that I missed and would like to see, I doubt I'd want to make that flight again. We left on Christmas Eve and arrived on Boxing Day. I guess that because neither of those days was Christmas Day, the airline declined to do anything special in the way of celebration or meals. It didn't win them any friends! It's just too long in 'cattle-car-class' for these old bones.

We grabbed a cab to our hotel in the Rocks, a neighbourhood that cozies up to the underside of the Sydney Harbour Bridge. The name of the hotel escapes me today, but it was half restaurant and half large B&B. It was fine. After a couple of days wandering around the city, we picked up a car and headed out. First stop was Katoomba and the Blue Mountains to see the "Three Sisters". First stop and first problem. The place was wall to wall fog. So much for that, so off to the Hunter Valley and a look around the oldest and highest regarded wine region of Australia at the time. Eventually we ended up at our friends' place in Newcastle where we spent a couple of days and participated in New Year's Eve celebrations with some of the local worthies in a neighbourhood called Merewether on a ridge overlooking the Pacific! A pretty impressive site if I may say so! After that we spent a couple of days working our way up the coast past Coffs Harbour and Byron Bay through the Gold Coast to Brisbane and ending up in a little town called Maroochydore on the Sunshine Coast of Queensland. On the way we stopped off at the Australia Zoo, the place made famous by the late Steve Irwin, The Crocodile Hunter. His family owns the Zoo and we were lucky enough to see Steve perform his show that day. Maroochydore marked the northern most limit of our travels. It's a nice town, with a good little Thai restaurant where we had supper. After that, it was on to Brisbane for a couple of days. As I don't remember much of it, the place obviously didn't excite me at the time.

Leaving Brisbane, we were off to the outback. We stopped in a place called Armidale, just south of the Gold Coast and got up early the next morning to head out when I got a call on my cell from one of the guys back in our agency with really terrible news I wasn't prepared for in any way. He'd been trying to reach me for a week to tell me that my mother had died in hospital the week before. A surprise like that sets you back a good bit. There was nothing we could do at that point but continue on. That's why I remember the name of a small town in the middle of Australia where I stayed one very quiet night. Our drive that day in a quiet car took us about 1,200 km to Broken Hill, New South Wales, right across the width of the state, right near the state line with South Australia and in a different time zone! The temperature that afternoon in January was in the 43C range, and the AC in our little no-tell-motel roared but still couldn't cool the place down. We had a private little wake that evening in a pure outback bar right out of a Crocodile Dundee movie. The door was a bead curtain, the place was rough, the inhabitants were rougher, clad with bush hats and singlets, the bartender brusque and the food was awful! The one good thing - cold beer! The next morning, we were up and on to Adelaide through a progressively more civilized and less daunting part of South Australia. We enjoyed the few days we spent in Adelaide as we were at a place by the ocean called Glenelg, a quaint, but growing prosperous seaside spot that was right on the tram line into downtown. It raised our spirits a bit.

We left Glenelg, and headed out for the Great Ocean road and the Twelve Apostles. We arrived in Melbourne and spent a few days wandering around, taking trams and exploring as far as St Kilda before our time was up. A quick flight over to Sydney then the long trip home to family and back to a funeral and then normal life! It was an easy trip to remember.

26.
EXPLORING THE CALIFORNIA COAST

HERE'S ONE way to see California, a bit of both north and south!

- Day 1 - Fly from Canada to San Francisco. If time allows, pick up a rental car and head to Napa Valley for an overnight stay at the Napa Valley Lodge (Yountville, just north of Napa on Route 29). Get reservations at the "French Laundry" for dinner, one of the best restaurants in California.

- Day 2 - Drive from Napa to Garberville, then on to Humboldt Redwoods State Park to the Avenue of the Giants. Stay at Myers Country Inn, one of the best small inns near the park.

- Day 3 - Visit the Redwoods then drive down Highway 101 to Highway 1 over to the wild Pacific coast and on to Mendocino for an overnight stay at the Mendocino Hotel & Garden Suites. Have dinner in the hotel.

- Day 4 - Leave Mendocino and head back via the old Highway 1 along the Pacific coast to San Francisco and over the Golden Gate Bridge and on to the Monterey area. If you enjoy the big city, check out the Embarcadero area of downtown San Francisco. Stay in the Carmel area. Believe it or not there's a great Best Western in the core of the town.

- Day 5 - Explore Carmel, Pebble Beach, and Monterey. Make a point of seeing the Aquarium in Monterey. Stroll down to the waterfront in Carmel and back to see how the other half lives.

- Day 6 - You can leave the Monterey area and drive down Highway 1, past Big Sur and onto the Hearst Castle at San

Simeon. Very much worth a visit. Plan to stay overnight just south of there in Moro Bay. Check out the Embarcadero Inn on the waterfront.

- Day 7 - Drive to Santa Barbara. Tonight, stay at the Fess Parker Santa Barbara Hotel (Double Tree Inn). Walk State Street and get to the Old Mission at Santa Barbara.

- Day 8 - Drive into L.A. and stay in either the Beverly Hills area or in Santa Monica. This is a day for shopping and star gazing. See the Crown Plaza Beverly Hills or the Avalon Hotel for places to stay.

- Day 9 - Find time to get to the tour of Paramount Studios. It's worth the visit. Allow a lot of time for getting from one place to another.

- Day 10 - If you used yesterday for Beverly Hills then today checkout Santa Monica and Muscle Beach and the Pier. When you're finished in Santa Monica, head down toward Laguna Beach. Stay at the Laguna Beach Inn tonight.

- Day 11 - Do Disney if you must, otherwise check out the Laguna Beach area.

- Day 12 - Day trip to San Diego. See Old Town, La Jolla, and the Zoo if you're into that.

- Day 13 - Keep your schedule clear of commitments. This is an open day, move it around if you like so you can fit it in what works for you.

- Day 14 - Your final day. Drive up to LAX airport and then fly home. Try to catch a mid-afternoon flight home so you don't have to fight the traffic on the Interstate 405! Hope you had a great trip!

27.

SOUTHERN CALIFORNIA PEOPLE

A WHILE back, we spent ten days in Southern California, an area we know reasonably well having spent a lot of time there over the years. We split our time between Laguna Beach and Santa Barbara with side trips to San Diego and Los Angeles. Rather than go on about where we stayed and what we saw and so forth, I'd like to take a few moments and introduce you to some of the people we met during our travels.

Laguna Beach is known as an artist haven and the reputation is still deserved, but no one is starving there today, that we saw. It's a quiet affluent community now. While we stopped at a number of galleries in town, two places made an impression on us.

One afternoon we stopped in the Laguna North Gallery and ended up talking with Margaret Jamison, a proponent of plein air painting. She was manning the gallery and working on a piece (indoors) and took a little time away from her brushes to stop and chat. Somehow we managed to kill the better part of three quarters of an hour just talking about the area and Margaret's work. A very pleasant woman who went out of her way to make us welcome. See her work at **www. margaretjamison.com**.

Ernie Jones was another artist who caught our ears and eyes. He's a member of an artist's cooperative a little further south in Laguna Beach called "Artist Eye Laguna Gallery". He and seventeen other artists are represented at the gallery, which is just across the street from the historic Hotel Casa del Camino built in 1928 and one of Laguna's current hot spots. One of the pieces that caught my eye as I entered the gallery was a giclée print on canvas reproduction of Ernie's triptych work called Sunset Rendezvous. The work is a realistic style painting of the hotel across the street! Again, we spent a little time talking to Ernie and enjoying the galleries various works. See his work at **www.artisteyegalleryla-guna.com**.

We had a day in the San Diego area planned to see the Zoo but first we would visit La Jolla for its galleries and shops. As fate would have it, as we were walking along in downtown La Jolla we got caught in a short tropical downpour and took cover under the awning of a local real estate office. We got caught dreaming about the multi-million-dollar estates that were featured in the office window by Steven Stocks, one of the agents in the office. He came out and joined us under the awning and we got talking. We enjoyed an entertaining and informative conversation about Southern California real estate markets. Steven was a real nice guy but we weren't in that real estate league! The rain slowed and we went on our way to see the seals on La Jolla Beach.

On to Santa Barbara and the Lavender Inn by the Sea where there's a meet and greet between four and six p.m. each evening. We had the chance to meet a couple of different people including a retired doctor from Kamloops named Jim Mabee. As an aside, our American cousins always seem to remark on the number of Canadians that visit their area of California. I'm not sure they understand real winter. Jim and his wife and Kathy and I spent an hour or so over glasses of wine talking about things. When dinnertime came, we walked around the corner to BJ's Brewhouse and enjoyed a noisy, busy meal during their open mic night. Local people of all ages filled the place and it was hopping. It was a fun start to our visit to Santa Barbara.

While the weather wasn't as warm as we'd hoped it would be, we had a fine time and enjoyed the opportunity to reacquaint ourselves with the Southern California lifestyle. Like many vacations, the most vivid highlights were some of the people we met during our wanderings. Our American neighbours are great hosts.

28.
HAWAII AND MAUI

AT ONE point I had a work colleague in Toronto who went to Hawaii every year for at least three weeks and he raved about the place. It was where he spent all of his time off. Kathy had been there a time or two, once on a business conference but became deathly ill from something she ate. I'd only heard stories and had never been there. Still we thought we'd give it a chance so we burned off some Aeroplan points and away we went. We've only made that one trip to Hawaii, besides a tech stop in Honolulu in both directions on a trip to Australia. It was a decade plus a few years back and while we enjoyed the break it wasn't a destination we'd do again.

Everybody has a preferred way to spend their leisure time and for us it doesn't normally include a lot of beach time. For most people, the islands of Hawaii and Maui are just that. At their best they offer sun, sea, and surf. That's just not us. We like getting out and exploring and that's what we did, but we found it left us with more down time than we wanted.

On the island of Hawaii, the best part of our stay was the day we picked up a rental car and drove around the east side of the island to the north shore and stopped at a number of spots, making it as far as Turtle Bay and Sunset Beach. We enjoyed seeing the massive surf and some surfers challenging the waves, but it soon lost its attraction. Our route back brought us through the middle of the island past the Dole Plantation and home to Honolulu. A few more days wandering Honolulu, drinking beer and hanging out was more than we needed.

The second part of the trip took us to Maui and, in some ways, we enjoyed it more. The towns in Maui were smaller and more intimate. This time, rather than a hotel we rented a condo near Lahaina and kept our expenses down by eating at home most days. We did find the islands expensive. Playing a round of golf at the time would have been cost prohibitive and possibly very embarrassing. Maui was more interesting as we visited the towns of Kaanapali and Kapalua and made two memorable road trips. The first one was a road trip to Hana on the east coast. It is famous for its tight narrow road and multiple tight turns and switchbacks. As a driver I found it fun and interesting, while I think Kathy was a little uncomfortable and tense. The village of Hana was intriguing and I would have stayed longer but I didn't want to drive the road back after dark. I understand the road has been extended well beyond Hana now and it can be a comfortable two day trip, particularly if someone else is doing the driving and guides you to some of the more beautiful wild spots on the coast. We also got part way up a mountain on another trip, but the weather started to get cloudy and cold so we called it a day and headed back to the beach!

As the old saying goes, to each their own. I know many people think Hawaii is the perfect place for them. That's not me, but if you go, enjoy the place for what it is.

29.
LET'S TRY FOR ANOTHER YEAR!

EACH YEAR on the 28th of May, I ask her if she wants to try for another year together! Normally, she says yes. After twenty-four of these question and answer sessions she said we should do it somewhere special for the next one. I agreed. The question was where. While the discussion started in late January, we had a hard time deciding. Nothing really caught our fancy. Finally, about mid April she was looking through a back issue of Travel & Leisure magazine when she noticed an ad for the 'Berkshires' area of western Massachusetts. It looked interesting to both of us, so we finally had our destination. We picked one of the hotels featured in the ad (who says advertising doesn't work!) and made a booking.

On Saturday, May 25th, away we went. After dropping our dog Princess off with Kathy's niece and spending an hour at the border crossing (it was Memorial Day weekend in the US), we were on our way. Six hours later we pulled up to the front of the hotel we booked, The Porches, as it is known, in the town of North Adams across from Mass MOCA. The hotel is a series of seven refurbished buildings that used to be houses for people who worked in the factory across the street. As the houses were repurposed into a hotel, the factory has become the Massachusetts Museum of Contemporary Art (Mass MOCA) and is one of the largest centres for contemporary visual and performing arts in the US. After check-in we headed out to get something to eat and then back to Mass MOCA for that evening's Aaron Neville concert. The concert was very enjoyable although Aaron's falsetto wasn't at its best, but that's understandable for a guy who's seventy-two and still out there. The surprise highlight of the concert was his brother Charles who is three years older and still playing a mean sax!

The next day after a busy breakfast off we went to explore the area. First stop was the Norman Rockwell Museum in Stockbridge, an hour's drive to the southern end of the area. This was one of the best little art galleries we've ever visited. It was a very pleasant way to spend a rainy morning seeing the work of an American icon. Well worth the visit.

The next stop was "The Mount", the house that American writer Edith Wharton spent ten of her best years building and improving. This was a bit of old hat for my wife, the ex-director of an historic house museum, but I still found it interesting. A not so quick lunch at the site of what used to be Alice's Restaurant (of Arlo Guthrie fame) and back on the road for a little shopping and just toddling around in a very pretty part of Massachusetts.

The next day (actual Memorial Day) was drier and off we went to The Clarke Art Institute in Williamstown. A small academically oriented collection of sixteenth to nineteenth century art. The property was under construction so only partially open to visitors. The gallery had a particular emphasis on Sargent and Renoir and was interesting but only worth an hour or so. A picturesque drive through the local highways and byways took us down to the village of Lenox where we arrived just as they were starting their Memorial Day ceremonies and parade. Being a fan of any parade she can find, Kathy was happy because we caught the perfect essence of small town (Rockwellian, even) America celebrating this national holiday. The high school band leading the local fire trucks and the aging veterans was picture perfect. Following this, we visited Ventfort House, another historic house museum of the Gilded Age. This one was nowhere as impressive as the one from the day before but it was still very much a work in progress according to the staff we talked to. After a late lunch at one of the highlight restaurants of the region (Atla) we meandered back to the hotel for a quiet evening in.

Our last full day in the area was our actual twenty-fifth and we had a celebratory meal planned for that evening. She surprised me by asking *me* if I wanted to try for another year! What the hell - why not! After a quiet breakfast, most of the weekenders and their 'rug rats' having left, we were on the road again. That morning we headed up Mount Greylock, the highest point in Massachusetts at over 3,700 feet. I'm sorry to report that it was a little underwhelming. However, it was a nice drive and from there we headed out on the local back roads to the Hancock Shaker Village near Pittsfield, the biggest town in the Berkshires. The Shaker Village is the site of a religious settlement that's been around for a couple of hundred years and finally died out in the first third of the twentieth century. The site has a lot of interesting information about this sect that believed in celibacy for its members and only found new members from volunteers and abandoned children. We wandered the site, visited the farm animals and had a nice lunch at their cafeteria. We finished the day with a very nice meal at the Gramercy Bistro at Mass MOCA to end our visit to the Berkshires. But wait… there's more!

The next day we headed home, hitting the road at ten a.m. and hoping to be home by four p.m., but it was not to be. An hour and twenty minutes out it was announced that a certain passenger had forgotten her purse in the breakfast room! A quick turnaround and back we went. We recovered the missing purse and were back at our turnaround point just outside Albany when the car decided to blow-up! It turned out that the water pump failed. We were lucky to find a Firestone service centre and they managed to get us back on the road within a couple of hours or so and lighter by more than a few hundred dollars! An hour later, we ran into one of the most intense storms we'd ever experienced in over forty years of driving. We were forced to pull over on the side of Interstate 90, along with most of the other traffic, and wait out the storm. Finally, we got back up to speed and eventually made it home, after picking up the Princess, at ten p.m., a full twelve hours after we started. All in all, I don't think either of us will ever forget our twenty-fifth anniversary.

30.
YOU CAN GO BACK!

WE'VE JUST returned from a most enjoyable short, big-city break. Twenty-five years ago, we lived in Toronto, a half block north of Queen Street, one block west of the Don River. Since returning to Ontario we had been staying away from the 'big smoke' as it felt just too difficult to get there. Also, if you follow the news, it can be none too pleasant if you did. Yet we didn't want to wander too far from home, nor spend US dollars, or be away for more than a few days. So, after a little bit of planning and a few weeks of waiting, off we went.

Rather than fight the QEW for two or three hours, we decided that once clear of the Burlington Skyway Bridge we'd slip down to Lakeshore Drive and cruise through the downtowns of Burlington, Oakville, Mississauga, Long Branch, New Toronto and Mimico. So doing, we enjoyed a serene mid-afternoon drive into our old hometown. Less than ninety minutes of relaxed meanderings later, we hopped onto the Gardiner for the last little bit into the city and off at Jarvis to the corner of Queen and Broadview in the east end.

Our destination was the new Broadview Hotel. In the bad old days, it was the home of Jilly's, an infamous east end strip joint in a building left over from the nineteenth century. A local developer bought the property a few years back and decided to take it from a sleazy old strip joint to a totally redone hipster hangout and hotel. He seems to have succeeded.

After checking in, we dropped our bags in our room (Room 604 - complete with LPs and a turntable, just like the old days). After stopping for a quick drink in the Café Bar we decided to stroll down Queen Street eastbound to see how things might have changed. We did stop for a couple of minutes in the first block to make a dinner reservation for later that evening. Our march took us back across the Don Valley Parkway and on down into our old neighbourhood, past the house we sold in 1994 at a loss, to move to Victoria (not many people in Toronto can say that now!) and eventually back to the hotel.

The reservation for supper that night was at Ruby Watchco, the creation of chef Lynn Crawford of TV fame. In fact Kathy was surprised when we went into the place to make the reservation that it was Ms. Crawford herself who took the reservation. After that pleasant experience, the meal turned out to be just the right thing for us. We chose the four-course prix-fixe menu and the matching wine, had a very good dinner, accompanied by good wine and music by a DJ that set just the right note for a couple of baby boomers. I'm glad the walk back to the hotel was only a half block!

The next morning was the start of a long day of walking about the core of Toronto. Our wandering took us down Queen Street, through some of the less salubrious parts of the city (Moss Park) and into the Eaton Centre (much changed since we left in 1994), past City Hall, up through Spadina Avenue's Chinatown, through Kensington Market and along College to Little Italy. A short stop at the Monocle Magazine retail outlet (to buy a couple of their European Travel Guides) and then back toward the city core for lunch at the slightly notorious Café Diplomatico and then it was en Marche! (With apologies to Emmanual Marcon). A walk through U. of T. and Queens Park brought us back to Yorkville. A large vibrant Ted Harrison painting in the window took me into Heffel's Gallery but the $25K price tag was well beyond what I could put out for my late, fellow Rotarian's work. If I had it to spare, I would have, but it was not to be. A final leg of our stroll took us to the AGO, but by then we were done, so it was into a cab (who's driver had become adept at U-turns on Bay Street - it's something about one way street problems) and back to the hotel for a refresher at the roof top lounge of the hotel (very popular and a place to see and be seen), before heading out to dinner with Kathy's cousin Patrick and his wife Ermalinda.

Dinner was in the Distillery District at a place called Cluny's French Bistro. It was a Wednesday evening and the various shops and restaurants were busy, yet there was no need for a reservation. After a good meal, catching up on family and listening to Pat's adventures from a holiday in Germany, it was a good walk home to the hotel.

The next morning after breakfast we decided to actually visit the AGO and walked down to the gallery. It had been awhile (decades) since we'd visited the gallery. We enjoyed the visit, particularly the Group of Seven works but had one more stop before heading home. We hopped on a Queen streetcar (actually a bus at this time as the streetcar tracks were under construction), went back to the hotel and checked out, got in the car (for the first time since we arrived) and headed for our last destination in Toronto for this trip. Unimaginably, we had an uninterrupted run up the DVP and westbound across the 401 to a place where friends of ours have found some really interesting furniture at a consign-ment store in the Yorkdale Shopping centre area. It's called "Of Things Past" on Bridgeland Ave. It carries an enormous selection of pre-owned furniture and fixtures of all manners and styles. Alas, nothing that we needed!

So, back on the 401 to the 403 to 407, the QEW and home to our quiet Niagara abode.

31.

NEWFOUNDLAND REUNION

BACK IN 1997, if you flew from Toronto to St. John's after connecting from Victoria, they got you there at about 4:30 a.m. or so. We got a cab to our hotel in the Mount Pearl area, and the driver was right out of Gordon Pinsent's "John and the Missus". A cab ride and entertainment included.

The real purpose of the trip was a family reunion on Kath's side. Her grandmother, on her mother's side was a Stentaford and that was the gathering clan. There were lots of family visits and long-lost cousins to reconnect with. It was a moving party with drop-ins all over and at least two large gatherings of the group with the main one being in the village of Brigus. It's a popular tourist stop, just across the water from Bay Roberts where that side of her family originally came from. I'm pretty sure there was no formal program as you'd have a hard time keeping these characters focused on anything but having a good chin wag! We were one of the furthest 'from away' participants, but there were two other members of the family from Vancouver Island. Mystery relatives, they had discovered the website, knew they were related and came. We had no clue they even existed. Kath certainly had never heard of them. None the less a good time was had by all.

Kathy's father was from St John's, but by the time we got there, only one uncle and a couple of aunts and a bunch of cousins were still with us and they were in the Beachy Cove area. The Summers family was one of the more successful groups from St. John's at one time, as it included a university professor, mayor of the city, an ambassador, lawyers and other business people. We made a stop to visit them and then carried on with the moving party.

You need to be well prepared for any visit to this part of the country. For example, a bunch of them went out whale watching early in the visit, but their digestive tracks weren't well prepared for the adventure. There is only so much Gravol can do to help, if you mix screech and ocean swells! You also need to know what the weather might be like for any visit. This gathering was at the end of July and the day we made a stop at an old graveyard in St. John's to drop in on some of the long-gone relatives we nearly froze to death! Always have a good coat with you when you visit our newest province.

We've not made a good effort since to get back. I don't know why, as it was the most enjoyable and fun time you can imagine. While many of the family may have passed, a return visit is on my agenda. She'd like to go again too, but will only allow it, if I promise good weather! If I had that type of luck, I'd be using it in Las Vegas!

32.
THE LAND OF THE 'NEWLY WED AND NEARLY DEAD' AND TOFINO

I'M BIASED; I lived there for fifteen years and enjoyed the time immensely. That's Victoria, B.C. I've also been to Tofino a number of times and that was just as enjoyable.

The 'Newly Wed and Nearly Dead' nickname came from the time when Victoria was a retirement community. That's no longer the case. Today it is a vibrant place to live, where all ages enjoy a milder climate than the rest of Canada and many opportunities to work in modern tech and other businesses and government and service industries. Mind you, the richest people there may be local real estate agents as it is one of the most attractive places to live in North America and the housing prices reflect that.

Living in Victoria is very good. For example, I am told there are more restaurants per capita than anywhere else in North America, except San Francisco. If you ride a bike, Victoria is the city for you. The weather allows year-round use and the bike infrastructure is very well developed. As a tourist town it also enjoys a number of cultural and entertainment attractions, including Craigdarroch Castle, the home built by the Bill Gates of his day, Robert Dunsmuir. He was a coal baron who had arrived in Canada with nothing and became the richest man in Western Canada before he died. He never did live in his castle, although the rest of his family did live there for a while. The tragedy in his story is he died before he could move in. The place was featured on the 'America's Castles' program a few years ago. Victoria is also known for its gardens, particularly Butchart Gardens, a year-round attraction for literally millions of people of all ages. It is fifty-five acres of gardens with over 900 varieties of plants set in five differently themed areas. Expect to spend at least four hours to see it all. My personal favourite garden is Abkhazi Gardens in Oak Bay with a very romantic tale of its founding. You would have no problem filling a week visit with things to do and see in the Victoria area. We still try to go back every couple of years to miss the Ontario winter for a few months and see old friends.

Four hours north and west of Victoria is Tofino, BC. This somewhat remote village in traditional native territory is for lovers of the great, and I mean great, outdoors! It is in a UNESCO Biosphere Region and has everything a big city doesn't! It has salt water; the settlement is on the edge of the Pacific, the next stop west being Japan. It has trees and rocks as it is in an old growth rainforest. It has native culture and an active artist colony to keep you busy. Stop by the Roy Henry Vickers Gallery in the village or any one of the other art outlets along the way. At various times we've stayed at the Red Crow guest house, The Long Beach Lodge Resort and Crystal Cove Beach Resort, among others. All were excellent. If you have a canine as a member of your family a Crystal Cove cabin is perfect for everyone. Book well in advance as this is one popular place year-round. Getting to Tofino may be the most challenging part of the trip as the road from Port Alberni to Tofino/Ucluelet is narrow, winding, steep and challenging and has too many fast-moving pickup trucks!

Vancouver Island is a place that anybody who likes to get away from a big city for a while will love. Give it a try. Be careful. You might want to stay!

33.
NOVA SCOTIA

WHILE I'VE been to the Halifax/Dartmouth area a number of times for business over the years, it's been almost forty years since I've been to Nova Scotia as a tourist. With any luck we will change that this coming summer (Covid 19 permitting) as we hope to head that way for a couple of weeks. We plan to drive there, and it will take us through New Brunswick, parts of which are quite familiar as I worked for one of the most prominent family businesses whose head office was in that province. Given the time gap since the last time, I still have some very strong memories of my last time down that way. I have a few favourites that I hope to see again.

I want to do the drive from Peggy's Cove along the shore to Yarmouth. All we saw the last time was fog! In fact, I saw nothing but fog in Yarmouth the day we arrived. The next morning it was clear as we headed out of town toward Digby and the Annapolis Valley, past Weymouth. The Valley was one of the prettiest little places on earth. I need to see it again to confirm that I wasn't just dreaming my memories. I know we took a rough road from Middleton over the hill to Margaretsville to see the Bay of Fundy and then back to the highway. It's worth seeing again. I'll bring a better camera with me this time.

From there, the next memorable stop will be Glace Bay and a visit to the Miner's Museum. I've been underground and as a person who's not comfortable in enclosed spaces it was slightly stressful. I still shudder a bit when I hear the Men of the Deeps singing with Rita McNeal the "Working Man" song. However, it's worth another visit. From there I want to see the Fortress of Louisburg, just down the road. Cape Breton seems to have a strong pull on me at this point in my life. Maybe it's because many of my ancestors are from that neck of the woods.

From there we'd loop back and take the Cabot Trail back toward Antigonish and maybe duck down and take the Eastern Shore drive again to Halifax and then head toward home. We'll still have a family visit to make on the way. We hope we can work out the timing because I have some new family members we need to make the acquaintance of.

On the way back we may even stop in the Berkshires region of Massachusetts, where we spent a very happy twenty-fifth anniversary some years ago!

Those are the plans anyway!

34.

OTTAWA

I GREW up in Ottawa and lived there until I was in my mid-twenties. My kid sister and her family still live there. I do have a soft spot for the place, but, boy has it changed. Still, it has a lot to offer to any visitor at any time of the year. I have pictures of myself before I left, skating on the Rideau Canal near the old DND Headquarters. Winterlude is the annual winter festival. Spring is usually one of the more colourful times of the year as the Dutch Royal family has been gifting tulips to the city since the Second World War in gratitude for sheltering the Dutch Princess Juliana from the Nazis. Summer, while shorter than some would like, attracts a large number of visitors to celebrate Canada Day, see the Changing of the Guard, wander through the Byward market and enjoy the galleries and national museums that are spotted about the city. There are Jazz and Blues festivals and the Sound and Light shows each night on Parliament Hill. The fall colours displayed from the local trees can be stunning!

Ottawa and the sister city of Gatineau across the Ottawa River have at least 1.3 million people, a lot more than when I left in the mid 70s. I grew up in what was in most respects a small city that's become a large bilingual Canadian metropolitan region. The Ottawa side is surrounded by a Green Belt where development is very limited, but it is growing quickly in suburban areas beyond the Green Belt.

For me it holds a lot of memories. I have a few old friends and army buddies still there and have been to at least one retirement party for an old soldier. The first and only home my parents bought is still there. My old schools are no longer schools but they are still in some form of use. While a lot has changed over the years the basic structure of the city still exists. The morning traffic jams on the Queensway still happen. The airport that marked the extreme south end of the city in my days is now surrounded by suburbs. I can remember as a kid riding my bike out to the airport on a two-lane Riverside Drive with gravel verges. We went to watch the aircraft take-off and land. I later worked there for a couple of years before leaving the city, yet if I go back now, I doubt I would recognize any of it. Today there are over twenty bridges to aircraft while in my day there may have been two and most people walked out to the tarmac to board their aircraft. From my point of view one of the best museums in the city is on the old defunct Rockcliffe air base in the east end of the city just before you get to the home of the RCMP's Musical Ride facilities. The Canadian Aviation and Space Museum is well worth the visit for anybody with an interest in aviation. My wife and I stopped by the last time we were in the city and our planned forty-five-minute visit lasted over two hours and it wasn't my entire fault!

Well, enough about my home town. Visit it if you get a chance, it will be well worth your time.

35.
WHERE I HAVEN'T BEEN!

AS YOU can see from the previous segments, I've been pretty lucky to experience a number of wonderful places. There are lots of spots I've missed during my travels and, at this point, I'm not likely to get to many of those. The most obvious reason is a lack of time and money. We, like most people, have limits on both and we had to say yes to some and no to a lot of others. Early on in the travel business I decided I would personally focus on what I knew and liked. I could, and did hire people who liked and knew other parts of the world. I also had to make some decisions about market interest in certain destinations. If west coast Canadians weren't going there, it was no use wasting money in trying to convince them otherwise. Here is a selection of destinations I've missed:

- Africa – It held little temptation for me and it was a small market from the west. I had a friend who worked for me and who travelled on business with me who came from Kenya and the stories he told tempted me. However, the time and resources weren't there. The beauty of South Africa was also tempting but, again, time and money got in the way.

- Asia – I have to admit this part of the world never much interested me. I can't explain this sentiment since the only obvious negative for me personally was the food. It just never was something I could bring myself to enjoy. Also, you can't do everything. We did have at least one other agent for a significant time who liked and actively sold that region.

- Antarctica – We have lots of cold and snow here in Canada. No need to go looking for it. I'm not really into adventure travel. I like the easy life.

- Mid-East – Maybe in quieter times, but the place has been an active war zone most of my life. In fact, at one point when I was a military officer, I was warned to be ready to take on the role of a logistic detachment commander in Herliya, Israel, which supported UN Peacekeepers on the Golan Heights. Things changed and nothing came of it. Just as well from my point of view.

- Eastern Europe – After the wall came down and the Soviet bloc crumbled, it might have been interesting, but some places just fell back into conflict and strife and it wasn't a good place to be as a visitor until recently.

I have to admit my interest in travel is to see parts of the world where people have been successful and have found ways to live together harmoniously. These are the places I want to visit and enjoy. If I wanted to see conflict and danger, I would have become a career soldier or a war correspondent/journalist, but I find writing hard work.

Happy travels to all.